50 Homemade Recipes for Home from Around the World

By: Kelly Johnson

Table of Contents

- Italian Margherita Pizza
- Japanese Sushi Rolls
- Mexican Chicken Enchiladas
- Indian Butter Chicken
- French Ratatouille
- Thai Green Curry
- Greek Spanakopita (Spinach Pie)
- Chinese Vegetable Stir-Fry
- Lebanese Falafel
- Brazilian Feijoada (Black Bean Stew)
- Moroccan Chicken Tagine
- Korean Bibimbap
- Spanish Paella
- Vietnamese Pho
- Turkish Baklava
- Jamaican Jerk Chicken
- Russian Borscht
- Ethiopian Doro Wat (Spicy Chicken Stew)
- Australian Pavlova
- Peruvian Ceviche
- Nigerian Jollof Rice
- Cuban Ropa Vieja
- Thai Mango Sticky Rice
- Italian Tiramisu
- Japanese Miso Soup
- Mexican Tacos al Pastor
- Indian Vegetable Biryani
- French Croque Monsieur
- Greek Moussaka
- Chinese Dumplings (Potstickers)
- Lebanese Tabbouleh
- Brazilian Coxinha (Chicken Croquettes)
- Moroccan Couscous
- Korean Kimchi
- Spanish Gazpacho

- Vietnamese Banh Mi
- Turkish Kofta Kebabs
- Jamaican Ackee and Saltfish
- Russian Pelmeni (Meat Dumplings)
- Ethiopian Injera (Sourdough Flatbread)
- Australian Meat Pie
- Peruvian Lomo Saltado
- Nigerian Pounded Yam and Egusi Soup
- Cuban Cubano Sandwich
- Thai Pad Thai
- Italian Risotto
- Japanese Tempura
- Mexican Chiles Rellenos
- Indian Palak Paneer
- French Crème Brûlée

Italian Margherita Pizza

Ingredients:

- Pizza dough (homemade or store-bought)
- 1-2 ripe tomatoes, thinly sliced
- Fresh mozzarella cheese, sliced or torn into pieces
- Fresh basil leaves
- Extra-virgin olive oil
- Salt and pepper, to taste
- Optional: garlic cloves, thinly sliced

Instructions:

1. Preheat your oven to the highest temperature it can reach, usually around 500°F (260°C). If you have a pizza stone, place it in the oven to preheat as well.
2. Roll out the pizza dough on a lightly floured surface into a round shape. Transfer the rolled-out dough to a piece of parchment paper.
3. Drizzle a little olive oil over the surface of the dough and spread it evenly with your hands or a pastry brush. If desired, scatter thinly sliced garlic over the oiled dough for extra flavor.
4. Arrange the tomato slices evenly over the oiled dough, leaving a small border around the edges.
5. Place slices or pieces of fresh mozzarella cheese on top of the tomato slices.
6. Tear fresh basil leaves and scatter them over the cheese.
7. Drizzle a little more olive oil over the pizza, then season with salt and pepper to taste.
8. Carefully transfer the parchment paper with the assembled pizza onto a baking sheet or preheated pizza stone in the oven.
9. Bake the pizza in the preheated oven for about 10-12 minutes, or until the crust is golden brown and the cheese is melted and bubbly.
10. Once done, remove the pizza from the oven and let it cool for a minute or two before slicing.
11. Slice the Margherita pizza into wedges or squares, and serve hot.

Enjoy your homemade Italian Margherita pizza, with its delicious combination of fresh tomatoes, creamy mozzarella, and fragrant basil leaves!

Japanese Sushi Rolls

Ingredients:

- Sushi rice (short-grain Japanese rice)
- Nori sheets (dried seaweed sheets)
- Assorted fillings (such as raw fish, cooked seafood, vegetables, avocado, cucumber, or tofu)
- Soy sauce, for dipping
- Wasabi paste, for serving
- Pickled ginger, for serving

Instructions:

1. Prepare the sushi rice according to package instructions. Rinse the rice under cold water until the water runs clear, then cook it according to the package instructions. Once cooked, let the rice cool slightly before using it to make sushi rolls.
2. Place a nori sheet shiny side down on a bamboo sushi rolling mat or a clean kitchen towel.
3. With wet hands, spread a thin layer of sushi rice evenly over the nori sheet, leaving a small border along the top edge.
4. Arrange your desired fillings horizontally across the center of the rice-covered nori sheet.
5. Starting from the bottom edge closest to you, carefully roll the nori sheet and rice over the fillings, using the bamboo mat or kitchen towel to help shape the roll. Apply gentle pressure as you roll to ensure the sushi roll holds together.
6. Once rolled, use a sharp knife to slice the sushi roll into individual pieces, about 1 inch thick.
7. Repeat the process with the remaining nori sheets, rice, and fillings until all the ingredients are used.
8. Serve the sushi rolls with soy sauce, wasabi paste, and pickled ginger on the side for dipping and garnishing.
9. Enjoy your homemade Japanese sushi rolls!

Feel free to get creative with your sushi roll fillings and combinations. You can also experiment with different sauces, toppings, and garnishes to customize your sushi rolls to your taste preferences. Have fun and enjoy the process of making and eating homemade sushi!

Mexican Chicken Enchiladas

Ingredients:

- 2 cups cooked shredded chicken (you can use rotisserie chicken or cook chicken breasts and shred them)
- 1 tablespoon olive oil
- 1 small onion, diced
- 2 cloves garlic, minced
- 1 can (14 ounces) diced tomatoes, drained
- 1 can (4 ounces) diced green chilies, drained
- 1 teaspoon ground cumin
- 1 teaspoon chili powder
- 1/2 teaspoon paprika
- Salt and pepper, to taste
- 1 cup enchilada sauce (store-bought or homemade)
- 8-10 small flour or corn tortillas
- 1 1/2 cups shredded cheese (cheddar, Monterey Jack, or a blend)
- Optional toppings: diced avocado, sliced jalapeños, chopped cilantro, sour cream, or salsa

Instructions:

1. Preheat your oven to 375°F (190°C). Grease a 9x13-inch baking dish with cooking spray or olive oil.
2. In a large skillet, heat the olive oil over medium heat. Add the diced onion and cook until softened, about 5 minutes.
3. Add the minced garlic to the skillet and cook for an additional minute, until fragrant.
4. Stir in the cooked shredded chicken, diced tomatoes, diced green chilies, ground cumin, chili powder, paprika, salt, and pepper. Cook for 5-7 minutes, stirring occasionally, to allow the flavors to meld together.
5. Spread a thin layer of enchilada sauce on the bottom of the prepared baking dish.
6. Place a spoonful of the chicken mixture in the center of each tortilla, then roll it up tightly and place it seam-side down in the baking dish. Repeat with the remaining tortillas and chicken mixture.
7. Pour the remaining enchilada sauce over the rolled tortillas, making sure to cover them evenly.

8. Sprinkle the shredded cheese over the top of the enchiladas.
9. Cover the baking dish with aluminum foil and bake in the preheated oven for 20-25 minutes, or until the cheese is melted and bubbly.
10. Remove the foil and bake for an additional 5 minutes, until the cheese is golden brown.
11. Once done, remove the enchiladas from the oven and let them cool for a few minutes before serving.
12. Serve the Mexican chicken enchiladas hot, garnished with your favorite toppings such as diced avocado, sliced jalapeños, chopped cilantro, sour cream, or salsa.

Enjoy these homemade Mexican chicken enchiladas as a delicious and satisfying meal!

Indian Butter Chicken

Ingredients:

For the marinade:

- 1 lb (450g) boneless, skinless chicken thighs or breasts, cut into bite-sized pieces
- 1/2 cup plain yogurt
- 1 tablespoon ginger-garlic paste (or finely minced ginger and garlic)
- 1 teaspoon ground cumin
- 1 teaspoon ground coriander
- 1/2 teaspoon turmeric powder
- 1/2 teaspoon Kashmiri red chili powder (or paprika, for color)
- 1/2 teaspoon garam masala
- 1/2 teaspoon salt

For the sauce:

- 2 tablespoons butter or ghee
- 1 onion, finely chopped
- 2 cloves garlic, minced
- 1-inch piece of ginger, grated
- 1 can (14 ounces) crushed tomatoes
- 1/2 cup heavy cream
- 1 teaspoon ground cumin
- 1 teaspoon ground coriander
- 1/2 teaspoon garam masala
- 1/2 teaspoon Kashmiri red chili powder (or paprika, for color)
- Salt, to taste
- Fresh cilantro, chopped (for garnish)

Instructions:

1. In a bowl, combine the yogurt, ginger-garlic paste, ground cumin, ground coriander, turmeric powder, Kashmiri red chili powder, garam masala, and salt.

Add the chicken pieces and coat them well with the marinade. Cover and refrigerate for at least 30 minutes, or preferably up to 4 hours.
2. In a large skillet or pan, melt the butter or ghee over medium heat. Add the chopped onion and cook until translucent, about 5-7 minutes.
3. Add the minced garlic and grated ginger to the skillet and cook for an additional 1-2 minutes, until fragrant.
4. Stir in the crushed tomatoes, ground cumin, ground coriander, garam masala, Kashmiri red chili powder, and salt. Cook the sauce for 8-10 minutes, stirring occasionally, until it thickens and the flavors meld together.
5. While the sauce is simmering, preheat your grill, grill pan, or oven broiler. Remove the chicken from the marinade and thread the pieces onto skewers if grilling.
6. Grill the chicken skewers or cook them in the grill pan or broiler until they are cooked through and lightly charred, about 6-8 minutes per side.
7. Once the chicken is cooked, add it to the simmering sauce along with the heavy cream. Stir to combine and simmer for an additional 2-3 minutes.
8. Taste the sauce and adjust the seasoning as needed, adding more salt or spices if desired.
9. Garnish the butter chicken with freshly chopped cilantro before serving.
10. Serve the Indian butter chicken hot with steamed rice, naan bread, or your favorite Indian bread.

Enjoy the rich and creamy flavors of homemade Indian butter chicken, a classic dish that's sure to delight your taste buds!

French Ratatouille

Ingredients:

- 1 large eggplant
- 2 medium zucchini
- 2 bell peppers (red, yellow, or orange)
- 4 ripe tomatoes
- 1 onion
- 3 cloves garlic
- 3 tablespoons olive oil
- 2 teaspoons dried herbes de Provence (or a mix of dried thyme, rosemary, and oregano)
- Salt and pepper, to taste
- Fresh basil leaves, for garnish (optional)

Instructions:

1. Preheat your oven to 375°F (190°C).
2. Wash and dice the eggplant, zucchini, bell peppers, and tomatoes into bite-sized pieces. Finely chop the onion and mince the garlic.
3. Heat 2 tablespoons of olive oil in a large skillet or Dutch oven over medium heat. Add the chopped onion and cook until softened, about 5-7 minutes.
4. Add the minced garlic to the skillet and cook for an additional 1-2 minutes, until fragrant.
5. Add the diced eggplant to the skillet and cook for 5 minutes, stirring occasionally.
6. Next, add the diced zucchini and bell peppers to the skillet, along with the dried herbes de Provence, salt, and pepper. Cook for another 5 minutes, stirring occasionally, until the vegetables start to soften.
7. Meanwhile, lightly grease a baking dish with the remaining tablespoon of olive oil.
8. Transfer the cooked vegetables from the skillet to the prepared baking dish, spreading them out evenly.
9. Arrange the diced tomatoes on top of the cooked vegetables in the baking dish.
10. Cover the baking dish with aluminum foil and bake in the preheated oven for 25-30 minutes, or until the vegetables are tender and cooked through.
11. Once done, remove the foil and bake for an additional 10-15 minutes, or until the liquid has reduced slightly.

12. Garnish the ratatouille with fresh basil leaves before serving, if desired.

Serve the French ratatouille hot or at room temperature as a side dish, appetizer, or main course. It pairs well with crusty bread, rice, pasta, or grilled meats. Enjoy the flavors of this classic French dish!

Thai Green Curry

Ingredients:

For the green curry paste:

- 2-3 green Thai chilies, chopped (adjust to taste)
- 2 shallots, chopped
- 3 cloves garlic, chopped
- 1 lemongrass stalk, chopped (white part only)
- 1 thumb-sized piece of galangal or ginger, chopped
- 1 tablespoon chopped cilantro stems
- 1 tablespoon chopped fresh basil leaves
- 1 tablespoon chopped fresh cilantro leaves
- 1 teaspoon ground coriander
- 1/2 teaspoon ground cumin
- 1/2 teaspoon ground white pepper
- 1/4 teaspoon ground turmeric
- Zest of 1 lime
- 2 tablespoons fish sauce
- 1 tablespoon soy sauce (or tamari for a gluten-free option)
- 1 tablespoon shrimp paste (optional, omit for a vegetarian/vegan version)
- 1 tablespoon coconut sugar (or brown sugar)
- Juice of 1 lime

For the curry:

- 1 tablespoon vegetable oil
- 1 can (14 ounces) coconut milk
- 1 cup vegetable broth
- 1 cup mixed vegetables (such as bell peppers, zucchini, carrots, and bamboo shoots)
- 1 cup cubed tofu, chicken, shrimp, or your choice of protein
- 2-3 kaffir lime leaves (fresh or dried)
- Fresh Thai basil leaves, for garnish
- Cooked jasmine rice, for serving

Instructions:

1. To make the green curry paste, combine all the ingredients in a food processor or blender. Blend until smooth, adding a little water if needed to help with blending.
2. Heat the vegetable oil in a large skillet or wok over medium heat. Add 2-3 tablespoons of the green curry paste (more or less depending on your desired level of spiciness) and cook for 1-2 minutes, until fragrant.
3. Stir in the coconut milk and vegetable broth. Bring the mixture to a simmer.
4. Add the mixed vegetables and protein of your choice (tofu, chicken, shrimp, etc.) to the skillet. Simmer for 5-7 minutes, or until the vegetables are tender and the protein is cooked through.
5. Add the kaffir lime leaves to the curry and simmer for an additional minute to infuse the flavors.
6. Taste the curry and adjust the seasoning as needed, adding more fish sauce, soy sauce, lime juice, or sugar to balance the flavors.
7. Remove the curry from heat and discard the kaffir lime leaves.
8. Serve the Thai green curry hot over cooked jasmine rice, garnished with fresh Thai basil leaves.

Enjoy the fragrant and flavorful Thai green curry, a comforting and satisfying dish that's perfect for any occasion! Adjust the spiciness and ingredients according to your taste preferences.

Greek Spanakopita (Spinach Pie)

Ingredients:

- 1 package (16 ounces) frozen chopped spinach, thawed and squeezed dry
- 1 cup crumbled feta cheese
- 1/2 cup grated Parmesan cheese
- 1/2 cup chopped fresh dill (or 2 tablespoons dried dill)
- 1/4 cup chopped fresh parsley
- 1 onion, finely chopped
- 3 cloves garlic, minced
- 4 tablespoons olive oil, divided
- Salt and pepper, to taste
- 1 package (16 ounces) phyllo pastry sheets, thawed
- 1/2 cup (1 stick) unsalted butter, melted

Instructions:

1. Preheat your oven to 375°F (190°C). Grease a 9x13-inch baking dish with cooking spray or olive oil.
2. In a large skillet, heat 2 tablespoons of olive oil over medium heat. Add the chopped onion and cook until softened, about 5 minutes.
3. Add the minced garlic to the skillet and cook for an additional 1-2 minutes, until fragrant.
4. Stir in the chopped spinach and cook for 3-4 minutes, until heated through. Season with salt and pepper to taste.
5. Remove the skillet from heat and transfer the spinach mixture to a large mixing bowl. Let it cool slightly.
6. Add the crumbled feta cheese, grated Parmesan cheese, chopped dill, and chopped parsley to the bowl with the spinach mixture. Stir until well combined.
7. In a small saucepan, melt the butter over low heat.
8. Unroll the phyllo pastry sheets and place them on a clean work surface. Cover them with a damp kitchen towel to prevent them from drying out.
9. Brush the bottom of the prepared baking dish with melted butter.
10. Place one sheet of phyllo pastry in the baking dish, allowing the edges to hang over the sides. Brush the phyllo sheet with melted butter.

11. Repeat the process with 5-6 more phyllo sheets, brushing each sheet with melted butter.
12. Spread the spinach and cheese mixture evenly over the layered phyllo sheets in the baking dish.
13. Fold the overhanging edges of the phyllo pastry over the top of the spinach mixture, creating a rustic border.
14. Layer the remaining phyllo pastry sheets over the top of the spinach mixture, brushing each sheet with melted butter.
15. Use a sharp knife to score the top layer of phyllo pastry into squares or triangles, being careful not to cut all the way through to the filling.
16. Bake the spanakopita in the preheated oven for 40-45 minutes, or until the phyllo pastry is golden brown and crispy.
17. Once done, remove the spanakopita from the oven and let it cool for a few minutes before slicing and serving.

Enjoy the delicious and flaky Greek spanakopita as a savory appetizer, side dish, or main course. It's perfect for brunch, lunch, or dinner, and leftovers can be enjoyed reheated or at room temperature.

Chinese Vegetable Stir-Fry

Ingredients:

- Assorted vegetables (such as bell peppers, broccoli, carrots, snap peas, mushrooms, bok choy, cabbage, onions, or any other vegetables of your choice), washed and chopped into bite-sized pieces
- 2 tablespoons vegetable oil (such as peanut, sesame, or canola oil)
- 2 cloves garlic, minced
- 1-inch piece of ginger, minced or grated
- Soy sauce, to taste
- Oyster sauce, to taste (optional)
- Salt and pepper, to taste
- Red pepper flakes or chili paste (optional, for heat)
- Sesame seeds, for garnish (optional)
- Cooked rice or noodles, for serving

Instructions:

1. Heat the vegetable oil in a large skillet or wok over medium-high heat.
2. Add the minced garlic and ginger to the skillet and cook for 1-2 minutes, until fragrant.
3. Add the chopped vegetables to the skillet, starting with the ones that take longer to cook (such as carrots and broccoli) and adding the quicker-cooking vegetables (such as bell peppers and snap peas) later.
4. Stir-fry the vegetables for 3-5 minutes, or until they are tender-crisp and brightly colored. Be sure to keep the vegetables moving constantly to prevent them from burning.
5. Season the stir-fry with soy sauce, oyster sauce (if using), salt, pepper, and red pepper flakes or chili paste (if using). Adjust the seasoning to taste.
6. Continue to stir-fry the vegetables for another minute or two, until they are evenly coated in the sauce and heated through.
7. Once done, remove the skillet from heat and transfer the stir-fried vegetables to a serving dish.
8. Garnish the Chinese vegetable stir-fry with sesame seeds, if desired.
9. Serve the stir-fried vegetables hot over cooked rice or noodles.

Enjoy your homemade Chinese vegetable stir-fry as a delicious and nutritious meal or side dish. Feel free to customize the recipe by adding your favorite protein (such as tofu, chicken, shrimp, or beef) or experimenting with different sauces and seasonings.

Lebanese Falafel

Ingredients:

- 1 cup dried chickpeas, soaked overnight (or use canned chickpeas, drained and rinsed)
- 1 small onion, roughly chopped
- 3 cloves garlic, minced
- 1/4 cup fresh parsley, chopped
- 1/4 cup fresh cilantro, chopped
- 1 teaspoon ground cumin
- 1 teaspoon ground coriander
- 1/2 teaspoon baking soda
- Salt, to taste
- Black pepper, to taste
- Vegetable oil, for frying

Instructions:

1. If using dried chickpeas, drain and rinse them after soaking overnight. If using canned chickpeas, drain and rinse them well.
2. In a food processor, combine the soaked or canned chickpeas, chopped onion, minced garlic, chopped parsley, chopped cilantro, ground cumin, ground coriander, baking soda, salt, and black pepper.
3. Pulse the mixture until it forms a coarse paste. You may need to scrape down the sides of the food processor bowl a few times to ensure all the ingredients are evenly mixed.
4. Transfer the falafel mixture to a bowl, cover, and refrigerate for at least 1 hour to allow the flavors to meld and the mixture to firm up.
5. After chilling, shape the falafel mixture into small balls or patties using your hands or a falafel scoop.
6. In a deep skillet or pot, heat vegetable oil over medium heat until it reaches 350°F (175°C).
7. Carefully drop the falafel balls or patties into the hot oil, working in batches to avoid overcrowding the pan.
8. Fry the falafel for 3-4 minutes, flipping them occasionally with a slotted spoon, until they are golden brown and crispy on all sides.

9. Once done, remove the falafel from the oil and transfer them to a plate lined with paper towels to drain excess oil.
10. Serve the Lebanese falafel hot with tahini sauce, hummus, tzatziki, or your favorite dipping sauce, along with pita bread and fresh vegetables.

Enjoy your homemade Lebanese falafel as a delicious and satisfying vegetarian meal or snack! You can also serve them as part of a mezze platter or in sandwiches or wraps.

Brazilian Feijoada (Black Bean Stew)

Ingredients:

- 1 lb (450g) dried black beans, soaked overnight
- 1 lb (450g) smoked pork sausage (linguiça), sliced
- 1 lb (450g) pork shoulder or pork belly, diced
- 1 lb (450g) beef brisket or beef ribs, cut into chunks
- 1 onion, chopped
- 4 cloves garlic, minced
- 2 bay leaves
- 1 tablespoon olive oil
- Salt and pepper, to taste
- Water
- Cooked white rice, for serving
- Orange slices, for serving
- Farofa (toasted cassava flour), for serving
- Chopped fresh cilantro, for garnish (optional)

Instructions:

1. Drain and rinse the soaked black beans. In a large pot, combine the black beans with enough water to cover them by at least 2 inches. Bring the water to a boil, then reduce the heat to low and simmer the beans, partially covered, for about 1 hour, or until they are tender but not mushy. Skim off any foam that rises to the surface.
2. In another large pot or Dutch oven, heat the olive oil over medium heat. Add the chopped onion and minced garlic, and sauté until softened and fragrant, about 3-4 minutes.
3. Add the sliced smoked pork sausage, diced pork shoulder or pork belly, and beef brisket or beef ribs to the pot with the onions and garlic. Cook, stirring occasionally, until the meats are browned on all sides, about 5-7 minutes.
4. Once the meats are browned, add the cooked black beans along with their cooking liquid to the pot. Add the bay leaves, and season with salt and pepper to taste.
5. Bring the feijoada to a simmer, then reduce the heat to low and let it simmer gently, partially covered, for 1-2 hours, or until the meats are tender and the

flavors have melded together. Stir occasionally and add more water if needed to keep the stew from drying out.
6. Once the feijoada is done cooking, remove the bay leaves and discard them.
7. Serve the Brazilian feijoada hot, accompanied by cooked white rice, orange slices, farofa, and chopped fresh cilantro, if desired.

Enjoy the rich and hearty flavors of homemade Brazilian feijoada, a beloved dish that's perfect for sharing with family and friends!

Moroccan Chicken Tagine

Ingredients:

For the Marinade:

- 4 bone-in, skin-on chicken thighs
- 2 cloves garlic, minced
- 1 teaspoon ground cumin
- 1 teaspoon ground paprika
- 1/2 teaspoon ground turmeric
- 1/2 teaspoon ground ginger
- 1/2 teaspoon ground cinnamon
- Salt and black pepper, to taste
- Juice of 1 lemon
- 2 tablespoons olive oil

For the Tagine:

- 2 tablespoons olive oil
- 1 onion, thinly sliced
- 2 cloves garlic, minced
- 1 teaspoon ground cumin
- 1 teaspoon ground paprika
- 1/2 teaspoon ground turmeric
- 1/2 teaspoon ground ginger
- 1/2 teaspoon ground cinnamon
- Pinch of saffron threads (optional)
- 1 cup chicken broth
- 1 cup canned diced tomatoes
- 1 cup green olives, pitted
- 1/4 cup chopped fresh cilantro, plus more for garnish
- 1/4 cup chopped fresh parsley, plus more for garnish
- Lemon wedges, for serving

Instructions:

1. In a bowl, combine the minced garlic, ground cumin, ground paprika, ground turmeric, ground ginger, ground cinnamon, salt, black pepper, lemon juice, and olive oil to make the marinade. Mix well.
2. Place the chicken thighs in a shallow dish and pour the marinade over them. Rub the marinade into the chicken thighs, making sure they are evenly coated. Cover the dish and let the chicken marinate in the refrigerator for at least 1 hour, or overnight for best results.
3. Heat 2 tablespoons of olive oil in a tagine or a large skillet with a lid over medium heat. Add the thinly sliced onion and cook until softened, about 5 minutes.
4. Add the minced garlic to the tagine and cook for an additional minute until fragrant.
5. Place the marinated chicken thighs in the tagine, skin side down, and sear them for 3-4 minutes until golden brown. Flip the chicken thighs and sear the other side for another 3-4 minutes.
6. Sprinkle the ground cumin, ground paprika, ground turmeric, ground ginger, ground cinnamon, and saffron threads (if using) over the chicken thighs.
7. Pour the chicken broth and canned diced tomatoes into the tagine. Stir to combine.
8. Cover the tagine and let the chicken simmer over low heat for 30-40 minutes, or until the chicken is cooked through and tender.
9. Add the pitted green olives, chopped fresh cilantro, and chopped fresh parsley to the tagine. Stir gently to incorporate the ingredients.
10. Remove the tagine from heat and let it rest for a few minutes before serving.
11. Garnish the Moroccan Chicken Tagine with additional chopped fresh cilantro and parsley. Serve hot with lemon wedges on the side.
12. Enjoy the flavorful Moroccan Chicken Tagine with couscous or crusty bread for a complete meal.

This Moroccan Chicken Tagine is sure to impress with its rich flavors and tender chicken, perfect for a special dinner at home.

Korean Bibimbap

Ingredients:

For the Bibimbap:

- 2 cups cooked short-grain white rice
- 4 cups assorted vegetables (such as spinach, carrots, bean sprouts, mushrooms, zucchini, and/or bell peppers), julienned or sliced
- 8 ounces beef (such as ribeye or sirloin), thinly sliced
- 4 large eggs
- Vegetable oil, for cooking
- Sesame oil, for drizzling
- Toasted sesame seeds, for garnish
- Thinly sliced green onions, for garnish

For the Gochujang Sauce:

- 1/4 cup gochujang (Korean chili paste)
- 2 tablespoons soy sauce
- 1 tablespoon rice vinegar
- 1 tablespoon sesame oil
- 1 tablespoon honey or brown sugar
- 2 cloves garlic, minced
- 1 teaspoon grated ginger
- 1 teaspoon toasted sesame seeds

Instructions:

1. Cook the short-grain white rice according to package instructions. Fluff the cooked rice with a fork and set aside.
2. Prepare the assorted vegetables by washing, peeling, and slicing them into thin strips or bite-sized pieces.
3. Heat a small amount of vegetable oil in a skillet over medium heat. Cook each type of vegetable separately, seasoning lightly with salt and pepper, until

tender-crisp. Remove each batch of cooked vegetables from the skillet and set aside.
4. In the same skillet, add a little more vegetable oil if needed and cook the thinly sliced beef until browned and cooked through. Season with salt and pepper to taste. Remove the beef from the skillet and set aside.
5. In the same skillet, fry the eggs sunny-side up or over-easy, until the whites are set but the yolks are still runny. Remove the eggs from the skillet and set aside.
6. To make the gochujang sauce, whisk together the gochujang, soy sauce, rice vinegar, sesame oil, honey or brown sugar, minced garlic, grated ginger, and toasted sesame seeds in a small bowl. Adjust the seasoning to taste.
7. To assemble the bibimbap, divide the cooked rice among serving bowls. Arrange the cooked vegetables and beef on top of the rice, leaving space for the fried egg.
8. Place a fried egg on top of each bowl of bibimbap.
9. Drizzle each bowl of bibimbap with sesame oil and the prepared gochujang sauce.
10. Garnish the bibimbap with toasted sesame seeds and thinly sliced green onions.
11. Serve the Korean Bibimbap hot, with extra gochujang sauce on the side for those who want it spicier.
12. To enjoy, mix everything together thoroughly before eating to combine all the flavors and textures.

Enjoy the delicious and colorful Korean Bibimbap as a satisfying meal that's packed with flavor and nutrition!

Spanish Paella

Ingredients:

- 2 cups bomba rice (or short-grain rice like Arborio)
- 4 cups chicken or vegetable broth
- 1 onion, finely chopped
- 4 cloves garlic, minced
- 1 red bell pepper, thinly sliced
- 1 green bell pepper, thinly sliced
- 1 yellow bell pepper, thinly sliced
- 1 cup green beans, trimmed and halved
- 1 cup frozen peas
- 1 tomato, grated
- 1 pinch saffron threads (optional)
- 1 teaspoon smoked paprika
- 1 teaspoon sweet paprika
- Salt and pepper, to taste
- 1 lemon, cut into wedges
- Fresh parsley, chopped, for garnish
- 1/4 cup olive oil

Optional protein additions:

- 8-10 large shrimp, peeled and deveined
- 8-10 small clams or mussels, scrubbed and cleaned
- 1 chicken breast, cut into bite-sized pieces
- 1 chorizo sausage, sliced

Instructions:

1. Heat the olive oil in a large paella pan or wide skillet over medium heat.
2. Add the chopped onion and minced garlic to the pan, and sauté until softened and translucent, about 3-4 minutes.
3. If using chicken or chorizo, add them to the pan and cook until browned and cooked through, about 5-6 minutes. If using seafood, skip this step for now.

4. Add the sliced bell peppers to the pan and cook for another 3-4 minutes, until slightly softened.
5. Stir in the green beans and grated tomato, and cook for another 2-3 minutes.
6. Add the bomba rice to the pan, and stir to coat the rice with the oil and vegetables.
7. Sprinkle the smoked paprika, sweet paprika, saffron threads (if using), salt, and pepper over the rice, and stir to combine.
8. Pour the chicken or vegetable broth into the pan, and bring to a simmer. Let the rice cook, without stirring, for about 10 minutes.
9. If using seafood, arrange the shrimp, clams or mussels over the rice, pressing them into the rice slightly. Cook for another 5-6 minutes, or until the seafood is cooked through and the clams or mussels have opened.
10. Scatter the frozen peas over the rice, and continue to cook for another 2-3 minutes, until the peas are heated through.
11. Remove the paella pan from heat, and cover it loosely with aluminum foil. Let the paella rest for 5 minutes before serving.
12. Garnish the paella with fresh parsley and lemon wedges before serving.
13. Serve the Spanish paella hot, directly from the pan, and enjoy!

Note: Traditional paella is cooked over an open flame, but you can easily make it on the stovetop. You can also customize this recipe by adding your favorite seafood, meat, or vegetables. Adjust the cooking time accordingly based on the protein you choose to include.

Vietnamese Pho

Ingredients:

For the Broth:

- 2 onions, halved
- 1 3-inch piece of ginger, halved lengthwise
- 4-5 pounds beef bones (such as oxtail, knuckle, or marrow bones)
- 1 cinnamon stick
- 3 star anise pods
- 3 cloves
- 1 cardamom pod
- 1 teaspoon coriander seeds
- 1 tablespoon salt
- 1 tablespoon sugar
- Water, enough to cover the bones (about 4-5 quarts)

For the Soup:

- 1 pound rice noodles (banh pho)
- 1 pound beef (such as flank steak, eye round, or brisket), thinly sliced
- 1 onion, thinly sliced
- 3-4 green onions, thinly sliced
- 1 cup bean sprouts
- Fresh Thai basil leaves
- Fresh cilantro leaves
- Fresh mint leaves
- Lime wedges
- Thinly sliced jalapeños or bird's eye chilies (optional)
- Hoisin sauce, for serving
- Sriracha or chili sauce, for serving

Instructions:

1. Char the onions and ginger: Preheat the broiler in your oven. Place the onion halves and ginger on a baking sheet and broil until charred, about 10-15 minutes. Turn them occasionally to ensure even charring. Alternatively, you can char them over an open flame on a gas stove.
2. Parboil the bones: Place the beef bones in a large stockpot and cover them with cold water. Bring the water to a boil over high heat, and let it boil vigorously for 10 minutes. This helps remove impurities from the bones and results in a clearer broth. Drain the bones and rinse them well under cold water.
3. Make the broth: In the same stockpot, add the parboiled bones, charred onions, charred ginger, cinnamon stick, star anise pods, cloves, cardamom pod, coriander seeds, salt, sugar, and enough water to cover the bones (about 4-5 quarts). Bring the water to a boil, then reduce the heat to low and let the broth simmer gently, uncovered, for at least 3-4 hours, preferably longer (up to 8 hours), skimming off any foam and fat that rises to the surface.
4. Strain the broth: Once the broth is done simmering, strain it through a fine-mesh sieve or cheesecloth into a clean pot or large bowl. Discard the solids.
5. Prepare the noodles: Cook the rice noodles according to the package instructions. Drain and rinse them under cold water to stop the cooking process and prevent them from sticking together.
6. Assemble the soup bowls: Divide the cooked noodles among serving bowls. Top them with thinly sliced raw beef, onion slices, and green onions.
7. Ladle the hot broth over the noodles and beef, ensuring that the beef is submerged in the hot broth. The hot broth will cook the thinly sliced beef.
8. Serve the pho: Serve the bowls of pho with bean sprouts, Thai basil leaves, cilantro leaves, mint leaves, lime wedges, and thinly sliced jalapeños or bird's eye chilies on the side. Let each person customize their bowl of pho with the desired toppings and condiments, such as hoisin sauce and sriracha or chili sauce.
9. Enjoy your homemade Vietnamese Pho hot and flavorful!

Note: Pho is a versatile dish, and you can customize it based on your preferences. Feel free to add other toppings such as cooked beef meatballs, sliced cooked beef tendon, or cooked tripe. You can also make a chicken version of pho (pho ga) by using chicken bones and meat instead of beef. Adjust the seasoning and spices to taste, and enjoy the rich and comforting flavors of homemade Vietnamese Pho!

Turkish Baklava

Ingredients:

For the Baklava:

- 1 package (16 ounces) phyllo dough, thawed
- 1 1/2 cups mixed nuts (such as walnuts, pistachios, and almonds), finely chopped
- 1 cup unsalted butter, melted

For the Syrup:

- 1 cup granulated sugar
- 1/2 cup water
- 1/2 cup honey
- 1 tablespoon lemon juice
- 1 cinnamon stick (optional)
- 3-4 whole cloves (optional)

Instructions:

1. Preheat your oven to 350°F (175°C). Lightly grease a 9x13-inch baking dish with butter or cooking spray.
2. Prepare the syrup: In a small saucepan, combine the granulated sugar, water, honey, lemon juice, cinnamon stick, and whole cloves (if using). Bring the mixture to a boil over medium heat, then reduce the heat to low and let it simmer for 10-15 minutes, stirring occasionally, until slightly thickened. Remove the cinnamon stick and cloves, if used, and set the syrup aside to cool.
3. Place the chopped nuts in a bowl and set aside.
4. Unroll the phyllo dough and cover it with a damp kitchen towel to prevent it from drying out.
5. Brush the bottom of the prepared baking dish with melted butter.
6. Place one sheet of phyllo dough in the bottom of the baking dish and brush it with melted butter. Repeat this process, layering and buttering the phyllo sheets, until you have used about half of the phyllo dough.
7. Sprinkle half of the chopped nuts evenly over the layered phyllo dough.

8. Continue layering the remaining phyllo dough sheets on top of the nuts, brushing each sheet with melted butter.
9. Sprinkle the remaining chopped nuts evenly over the top layer of phyllo dough.
10. Using a sharp knife, carefully cut the baklava into diamond or square shapes, being careful not to cut all the way through to the bottom of the baking dish.
11. Bake the baklava in the preheated oven for 30-35 minutes, or until the phyllo dough is golden brown and crisp.
12. Remove the baklava from the oven and immediately pour the cooled syrup evenly over the hot baklava, allowing it to soak in completely.
13. Let the baklava cool to room temperature in the baking dish before serving.
14. Enjoy your homemade Turkish baklava, with its layers of crispy phyllo dough, crunchy nuts, and sweet syrup, as a delicious and decadent dessert!

Note: Baklava is best enjoyed within a few days of baking. Store any leftovers in an airtight container at room temperature.

Jamaican Jerk Chicken

Ingredients:

For the Jerk Marinade:

- 3-4 pounds chicken pieces (such as thighs, drumsticks, or breast)
- 1/4 cup green onions (scallions), chopped
- 4 cloves garlic, minced
- 2-3 Scotch bonnet peppers (or habanero peppers), seeded and chopped (adjust to taste)
- 1 tablespoon fresh thyme leaves
- 2 teaspoons ground allspice
- 2 teaspoons ground black pepper
- 2 teaspoons ground cinnamon
- 2 teaspoons ground nutmeg
- 2 teaspoons ground ginger
- 2 teaspoons brown sugar or granulated sugar
- 2 tablespoons soy sauce or tamari
- 2 tablespoons olive oil
- 2 tablespoons vinegar (apple cider vinegar or white vinegar)
- Juice of 2 limes
- Salt, to taste

Instructions:

1. In a blender or food processor, combine the green onions, minced garlic, chopped Scotch bonnet peppers, fresh thyme leaves, ground allspice, ground black pepper, ground cinnamon, ground nutmeg, ground ginger, brown sugar, soy sauce, olive oil, vinegar, lime juice, and salt. Blend until smooth to make the jerk marinade.
2. Place the chicken pieces in a large bowl or resealable plastic bag. Pour the jerk marinade over the chicken, making sure each piece is well coated. Cover the bowl or seal the bag, and refrigerate the chicken to marinate for at least 4 hours, or overnight for best results.
3. Preheat your grill to medium-high heat, or preheat your oven to 375°F (190°C).

4. If grilling, lightly oil the grill grates to prevent sticking. Remove the chicken from the marinade and shake off any excess marinade. Grill the chicken over medium-high heat, turning occasionally, until it is cooked through and has grill marks on both sides, about 20-25 minutes for thighs and drumsticks, or 15-20 minutes for breasts. If roasting, place the chicken on a baking sheet lined with parchment paper or aluminum foil and roast in the preheated oven until cooked through, about 25-30 minutes for thighs and drumsticks, or 20-25 minutes for breasts.
5. Once done, transfer the cooked Jamaican Jerk Chicken to a serving platter and let it rest for a few minutes before serving.
6. Serve the Jamaican Jerk Chicken hot, with rice and peas, fried plantains, or your favorite sides. Garnish with additional fresh thyme leaves or chopped green onions, if desired.

Enjoy the bold and spicy flavors of homemade Jamaican Jerk Chicken, a delicious and iconic dish that's perfect for summer grilling or any time of the year!

Russian Borscht

Ingredients:

- 2 tablespoons olive oil or vegetable oil
- 1 onion, diced
- 2 carrots, diced
- 2 celery stalks, diced
- 3-4 medium beets, peeled and grated
- 2 potatoes, peeled and diced
- 4 cups beef or vegetable broth
- 1 (14.5-ounce) can diced tomatoes, undrained
- 2 cloves garlic, minced
- 1 bay leaf
- 1 teaspoon dried dill (or 1 tablespoon fresh dill, chopped)
- Salt and pepper, to taste
- 2 tablespoons red wine vinegar or apple cider vinegar
- Sour cream, for serving
- Fresh dill, chopped, for garnish
- Crusty bread, for serving (optional)

Instructions:

1. Heat the olive oil or vegetable oil in a large soup pot or Dutch oven over medium heat. Add the diced onion, carrots, and celery, and sauté for 5-7 minutes, or until the vegetables are softened.
2. Add the grated beets and diced potatoes to the pot, and sauté for another 5 minutes, stirring occasionally.
3. Pour the beef or vegetable broth into the pot, along with the diced tomatoes (including their juices), minced garlic, bay leaf, and dried dill. Season with salt and pepper to taste.
4. Bring the soup to a simmer, then reduce the heat to low and let it simmer, partially covered, for 30-40 minutes, or until the vegetables are tender.
5. Stir in the red wine vinegar or apple cider vinegar, and adjust the seasoning if needed.
6. Remove the bay leaf from the soup and discard it.

7. Ladle the hot borscht into serving bowls. Serve the borscht hot, topped with a dollop of sour cream and a sprinkle of fresh chopped dill. Serve with crusty bread on the side, if desired.
8. Enjoy your homemade Russian Borscht as a comforting and hearty soup, perfect for a cold winter day or any time you're craving a taste of Russian cuisine!

Note: You can customize this borscht recipe by adding other vegetables such as cabbage, bell peppers, or beans. You can also add cooked beef or sausage for extra protein. Adjust the cooking time accordingly if adding additional ingredients.

Ethiopian Doro Wat (Spicy Chicken Stew)

Ingredients:

For the Spice Blend (Berbere):

- 2 tablespoons paprika
- 1 tablespoon ground cayenne pepper (adjust to taste for desired level of spiciness)
- 1 tablespoon ground coriander
- 1 tablespoon ground fenugreek
- 1 tablespoon ground cumin
- 1 tablespoon ground cardamom
- 1 tablespoon ground black pepper
- 1 teaspoon ground cloves
- 1 teaspoon ground allspice
- 1 teaspoon ground cinnamon
- 1 teaspoon ground nutmeg
- 1 teaspoon turmeric
- 1 teaspoon salt

For the Doro Wat:

- 2 tablespoons clarified butter (niter kibbeh) or olive oil
- 1 large onion, finely chopped
- 3 cloves garlic, minced
- 1 tablespoon fresh ginger, minced
- 2 tablespoons berbere spice blend (adjust to taste)
- 2 pounds chicken pieces (such as thighs and drumsticks), skin-on
- 2 cups chicken broth
- 2 tablespoons tomato paste
- 2 tablespoons lemon juice
- Salt, to taste
- Hard-boiled eggs, peeled (optional)
- Fresh cilantro, chopped, for garnish (optional)
- Injera or rice, for serving

Instructions:

1. Prepare the berbere spice blend: In a small bowl, combine all the spices listed under "Spice Blend (Berbere)." Mix well to combine. This spice blend can be stored in an airtight container for future use.
2. Heat the clarified butter or olive oil in a large Dutch oven or heavy-bottomed pot over medium heat.
3. Add the chopped onion to the pot and sauté until softened and translucent, about 5-7 minutes.
4. Stir in the minced garlic, minced ginger, and berbere spice blend. Cook for another 2-3 minutes, stirring constantly, until fragrant.
5. Add the chicken pieces to the pot and coat them evenly with the spice mixture.
6. Pour the chicken broth into the pot, along with the tomato paste and lemon juice. Stir to combine.
7. Bring the mixture to a simmer, then reduce the heat to low. Cover the pot and let the Doro Wat simmer gently for about 45-60 minutes, or until the chicken is cooked through and tender, and the flavors have melded together. Stir occasionally and add more chicken broth if needed to prevent the stew from drying out.
8. Taste the Doro Wat and adjust the seasoning with salt if needed.
9. If using hard-boiled eggs, gently nestle them into the stew, making sure they are submerged in the sauce.
10. Serve the Ethiopian Doro Wat hot, garnished with chopped fresh cilantro, if desired. Serve with injera or rice on the side for soaking up the flavorful sauce.
11. Enjoy your homemade Ethiopian Doro Wat, a delicious and aromatic chicken stew that's perfect for sharing with family and friends!

Australian Pavlova

Ingredients:

For the Meringue:

- 4 large egg whites, at room temperature
- 1 cup granulated sugar
- 1 teaspoon cornstarch
- 1 teaspoon white vinegar
- 1 teaspoon vanilla extract

For the Topping:

- 1 cup heavy cream, chilled
- 2 tablespoons powdered sugar
- Fresh fruit (such as strawberries, kiwi, passionfruit, or berries), sliced or chopped, for topping

Instructions:

1. Preheat your oven to 250°F (120°C). Line a baking sheet with parchment paper.
2. In a clean, dry mixing bowl, beat the egg whites with an electric mixer on medium speed until soft peaks form.
3. Gradually add the granulated sugar, 1 tablespoon at a time, while continuing to beat the egg whites. Once all the sugar has been added, increase the speed to high and beat until stiff peaks form and the meringue is glossy and thick.
4. Sprinkle the cornstarch over the meringue, then add the white vinegar and vanilla extract. Gently fold them into the meringue using a spatula until evenly incorporated.
5. Spoon the meringue onto the prepared baking sheet, forming a circle or oval shape with slightly raised edges to hold the filling.
6. Place the baking sheet in the preheated oven and bake the meringue for 1 hour and 15 minutes to 1 hour and 30 minutes, or until the outside is crisp and dry, but the inside is still soft and marshmallow-like. The meringue should be lightly

golden on the outside. Turn off the oven and let the meringue cool completely in the oven with the door closed, preferably overnight.
7. Just before serving, whip the chilled heavy cream with powdered sugar until soft peaks form.
8. Carefully transfer the cooled meringue to a serving platter. Spread the whipped cream evenly over the top of the meringue.
9. Arrange the sliced or chopped fresh fruit on top of the whipped cream.
10. Serve the Australian Pavlova immediately, as the meringue may soften over time once topped with cream and fruit.
11. Enjoy the light and airy texture of the meringue paired with the creamy whipped cream and sweet, juicy fruit in this classic Australian dessert!

Note: Pavlova is best enjoyed on the day it is assembled, as the meringue can become soft if stored for too long with the cream and fruit.

Peruvian Ceviche

Ingredients:

- 1 pound firm white fish fillets (such as tilapia, halibut, or sea bass), cut into bite-sized pieces
- 1 cup freshly squeezed lime juice (about 8-10 limes)
- 1 red onion, thinly sliced
- 1-2 fresh chili peppers (such as jalapeño or serrano), seeded and finely chopped
- 1-2 cloves garlic, minced
- 1 tablespoon fresh cilantro, chopped
- Salt, to taste
- Freshly ground black pepper, to taste
- 1-2 ears of fresh corn, cooked and kernels removed (optional)
- 1-2 sweet potatoes, boiled and sliced (optional)
- Lettuce leaves or corn nuts, for serving (optional)

Instructions:

1. In a large non-metallic bowl, combine the bite-sized pieces of fish with the freshly squeezed lime juice. Make sure the fish is completely submerged in the lime juice. Cover the bowl and refrigerate for at least 30 minutes to 1 hour, or until the fish is "cooked" by the acidity of the lime juice. The fish will turn opaque and firm when it's ready.
2. While the fish is marinating, prepare the other ingredients. Thinly slice the red onion, chop the fresh chili peppers, mince the garlic, and chop the fresh cilantro.
3. Once the fish is "cooked" in the lime juice, drain off most of the lime juice, leaving just enough to keep the ceviche moist.
4. Add the thinly sliced red onion, chopped chili peppers, minced garlic, chopped cilantro, salt, and freshly ground black pepper to the bowl with the fish. Gently toss everything together to combine.
5. Taste the ceviche and adjust the seasoning if needed, adding more salt or pepper as desired.
6. If using, add the cooked corn kernels to the ceviche and toss to combine.
7. To serve, divide the Peruvian ceviche among serving plates or bowls. You can serve it on a bed of lettuce leaves or garnish it with corn nuts for added texture and crunch.

8. Optionally, serve the ceviche with boiled sweet potato slices on the side to balance the acidity of the dish.
9. Enjoy your homemade Peruvian ceviche immediately as a refreshing appetizer or light meal, perfect for a hot summer day or any time you're craving the bright flavors of Peru!

Note: It's important to use fresh, high-quality fish for ceviche, as it will be consumed raw. Ensure that the fish is sourced from a reputable supplier and has been properly handled and stored. Additionally, consume the ceviche within a day of making it for the best taste and texture.

Nigerian Jollof Rice

Ingredients:

- 2 cups long-grain parboiled rice
- 1/4 cup vegetable oil or palm oil
- 1 onion, finely chopped
- 3-4 cloves garlic, minced
- 1 bell pepper (red or green), finely chopped
- 1-2 Scotch bonnet peppers (or habanero peppers), seeded and finely chopped (adjust to taste)
- 1 can (14.5 ounces) crushed tomatoes
- 1 tablespoon tomato paste
- 1 teaspoon paprika
- 1 teaspoon thyme
- 1 teaspoon curry powder
- 1 teaspoon ground cayenne pepper (optional, for extra heat)
- 2 cups chicken or vegetable broth
- Salt, to taste
- Freshly ground black pepper, to taste
- Fresh parsley or cilantro, chopped, for garnish (optional)

Instructions:

1. Rinse the parboiled rice under cold water until the water runs clear. Drain and set aside.
2. Heat the vegetable oil or palm oil in a large pot or Dutch oven over medium heat.
3. Add the chopped onion to the pot and sauté until softened and translucent, about 5-7 minutes.
4. Stir in the minced garlic, chopped bell pepper, and chopped Scotch bonnet peppers. Cook for another 2-3 minutes, until the peppers are softened.
5. Add the crushed tomatoes and tomato paste to the pot, along with the paprika, thyme, curry powder, and ground cayenne pepper (if using). Stir to combine.
6. Cook the tomato mixture for 5-7 minutes, stirring occasionally, until the flavors are well combined and the sauce has thickened slightly.
7. Pour the chicken or vegetable broth into the pot and bring the mixture to a boil.

8. Stir in the rinsed parboiled rice, making sure it's evenly distributed in the pot and submerged in the liquid. Season with salt and freshly ground black pepper to taste.
9. Reduce the heat to low, cover the pot, and let the Jollof Rice simmer gently for about 20-25 minutes, or until the rice is tender and has absorbed all the liquid. Stir the rice occasionally to prevent it from sticking to the bottom of the pot.
10. Once the rice is cooked, remove the pot from the heat and let it sit, covered, for 5 minutes to steam.
11. Fluff the Jollof Rice with a fork to separate the grains.
12. Serve the Nigerian Jollof Rice hot, garnished with chopped fresh parsley or cilantro if desired.
13. Enjoy your homemade Nigerian Jollof Rice as a flavorful and satisfying main dish or side dish, perfect for sharing with family and friends at any gathering or celebration!

Cuban Ropa Vieja

Ingredients:

- 2 pounds flank steak or skirt steak
- Salt and pepper, to taste
- 2 tablespoons olive oil
- 1 onion, thinly sliced
- 1 green bell pepper, thinly sliced
- 1 red bell pepper, thinly sliced
- 3 cloves garlic, minced
- 1 can (14.5 ounces) diced tomatoes, undrained
- 1 can (6 ounces) tomato paste
- 1 cup beef broth
- 1 teaspoon ground cumin
- 1 teaspoon dried oregano
- 1 bay leaf
- 1/4 cup chopped fresh cilantro or parsley, for garnish
- Cooked white rice, for serving
- Fried plantains or black beans, for serving (optional)

Instructions:

1. Season the flank steak or skirt steak generously with salt and pepper on both sides.
2. Heat the olive oil in a large Dutch oven or heavy-bottomed pot over medium-high heat. Add the seasoned steak to the pot and sear it on both sides until browned, about 3-4 minutes per side. Remove the steak from the pot and set it aside.
3. In the same pot, add the thinly sliced onion, green bell pepper, and red bell pepper. Cook, stirring occasionally, until the vegetables are softened, about 5-7 minutes.
4. Stir in the minced garlic and cook for another 1-2 minutes, until fragrant.
5. Return the seared steak to the pot. Add the diced tomatoes, tomato paste, beef broth, ground cumin, dried oregano, and bay leaf to the pot. Stir to combine.
6. Bring the mixture to a simmer, then reduce the heat to low. Cover the pot and let the Ropa Vieja simmer gently for 2-3 hours, or until the steak is very tender and easily shreds with a fork.

7. Once the steak is cooked, remove it from the pot and transfer it to a cutting board. Use two forks to shred the steak into bite-sized pieces.
8. Return the shredded steak to the pot and stir it into the sauce. Simmer the Ropa Vieja uncovered for another 10-15 minutes to allow the flavors to meld together and the sauce to thicken slightly.
9. Taste the Ropa Vieja and adjust the seasoning with salt and pepper if needed.
10. Garnish the Cuban Ropa Vieja with chopped fresh cilantro or parsley before serving.
11. Serve the Ropa Vieja hot, over cooked white rice, with fried plantains or black beans on the side if desired.
12. Enjoy your homemade Cuban Ropa Vieja, a comforting and flavorful dish that's perfect for sharing with family and friends!

Thai Mango Sticky Rice

Ingredients:

For the Sticky Rice:

- 1 cup glutinous rice (also called sticky rice or sweet rice)
- 1 cup coconut milk
- 1/2 cup granulated sugar
- 1/2 teaspoon salt
- 1 pandan leaf (optional, for aroma)

For Serving:

- 2 ripe mangoes, peeled and sliced
- 1/2 cup coconut milk
- 2 tablespoons granulated sugar
- A pinch of salt
- Toasted sesame seeds or toasted mung beans (optional, for garnish)

Instructions:

1. Rinse the glutinous rice under cold water until the water runs clear. Soak the rice in water for at least 4 hours or overnight.
2. Drain the soaked rice and transfer it to a steamer basket lined with cheesecloth or a clean kitchen towel. Steam the rice over medium heat for 20-25 minutes, or until tender and cooked through.
3. While the rice is steaming, prepare the coconut sauce. In a small saucepan, combine the coconut milk, granulated sugar, and salt. Heat the mixture over medium heat, stirring constantly, until the sugar has dissolved and the sauce is smooth. Remove the saucepan from the heat and set aside.
4. Once the rice is cooked, transfer it to a mixing bowl. Pour the coconut milk mixture over the cooked rice while it's still warm. Stir gently to coat the rice evenly with the coconut sauce. Let the rice sit for 10-15 minutes to absorb the coconut sauce and become sticky.

5. While the rice is resting, prepare the mangoes. Peel the mangoes and slice them into thin strips or cubes.
6. To serve, divide the sticky rice among serving plates or bowls. Arrange the sliced mangoes on top or alongside the rice.
7. Drizzle additional coconut sauce over the mangoes and rice, if desired. Garnish with toasted sesame seeds or toasted mung beans, if using.
8. Serve the Thai Mango Sticky Rice warm or at room temperature.
9. Enjoy the delicious combination of sweet, sticky rice with ripe mangoes and creamy coconut sauce, a popular and refreshing dessert in Thai cuisine!

Note: If pandan leaves are available, you can tie them into a knot and add them to the coconut milk mixture while heating to infuse the sauce with a subtle aroma. If you don't have a steamer, you can cook the soaked rice in a rice cooker or on the stovetop using the absorption method. Adjust the sweetness of the coconut sauce according to your preference.

Italian Tiramisu

Ingredients:

- 1 cup strong brewed coffee, cooled to room temperature
- 2 tablespoons coffee liqueur (such as Kahlua), optional
- 24-30 ladyfinger biscuits (savoiardi)
- 4 large eggs, separated
- 1 cup granulated sugar, divided
- 16 ounces (about 2 cups) mascarpone cheese, softened
- 1 teaspoon vanilla extract
- Cocoa powder, for dusting

Instructions:

1. In a shallow dish, mix the brewed coffee with the coffee liqueur (if using). Set aside.
2. In a large mixing bowl, beat the egg yolks with 1/2 cup of granulated sugar until pale and thickened. Add the softened mascarpone cheese and vanilla extract, and beat until smooth and creamy. Set aside.
3. In another large mixing bowl, beat the egg whites with the remaining 1/2 cup of granulated sugar until stiff peaks form.
4. Gently fold the beaten egg whites into the mascarpone mixture until well combined. Be careful not to deflate the egg whites.
5. Dip each ladyfinger biscuit into the coffee mixture for about 1-2 seconds on each side, ensuring they are soaked but not overly soggy.
6. Arrange a layer of soaked ladyfinger biscuits in the bottom of a 9x13-inch dish or a similar-sized serving dish.
7. Spread half of the mascarpone mixture evenly over the soaked ladyfinger biscuits.
8. Repeat the layers: Arrange another layer of soaked ladyfinger biscuits on top of the mascarpone mixture, followed by the remaining mascarpone mixture.
9. Cover the dish with plastic wrap and refrigerate the tiramisu for at least 4 hours, or overnight, to allow the flavors to meld together and the dessert to set.
10. Before serving, sift cocoa powder evenly over the top of the chilled tiramisu.
11. Slice and serve the Italian Tiramisu cold, with a dusting of cocoa powder on top of each serving.

12. Enjoy the creamy, indulgent layers of coffee-soaked biscuits and mascarpone cheese in this classic Italian dessert!

Note: Traditional tiramisu is made with raw eggs. If you're concerned about consuming raw eggs, you can use pasteurized eggs or substitute them with an eggless tiramisu recipe. Additionally, you can adjust the sweetness of the dessert by reducing or increasing the amount of sugar according to your preference.

Japanese Miso Soup

Ingredients:

- 4 cups water
- 2 tablespoons dashi granules (or 4 cups prepared dashi stock)
- 3 tablespoons miso paste (white or red)
- 4 ounces tofu, cut into small cubes
- 2 green onions, thinly sliced
- 1 sheet nori (seaweed), cut into small pieces (optional)
- 1 tablespoon soy sauce (optional)
- 1 tablespoon mirin (optional)
- Cooked rice, for serving (optional)

Instructions:

1. In a medium pot, bring the water to a simmer over medium heat. If using dashi granules, dissolve them in the simmering water to make dashi stock.
2. Once the dashi stock is ready, reduce the heat to low and add the tofu cubes to the pot. Let them simmer gently for 2-3 minutes to heat through.
3. In a small bowl, whisk together the miso paste with a ladleful of the hot dashi broth until smooth.
4. Add the miso mixture to the pot and stir well to combine. Be careful not to boil the miso soup once the miso paste has been added, as boiling can destroy its flavor.
5. Add the sliced green onions and nori pieces to the pot, stirring gently.
6. Taste the miso soup and adjust the seasoning if needed. You can add soy sauce or mirin for additional flavor, if desired.
7. Remove the pot from the heat and ladle the miso soup into serving bowls.
8. Serve the Japanese Miso Soup hot, alongside cooked rice if desired.
9. Enjoy your homemade miso soup as a comforting and nutritious appetizer or light meal, perfect for any time of the day!

Note: Feel free to customize your miso soup with other ingredients like mushrooms, spinach, or wakame seaweed. Adjust the amount of miso paste according to your preference for saltiness.

Mexican Tacos al Pastor

Ingredients:

For the Marinade:

- 4 dried guajillo chilies, stemmed and seeded
- 2 dried ancho chilies, stemmed and seeded
- 1/2 cup pineapple juice
- 4 cloves garlic, minced
- 1 tablespoon ground cumin
- 1 tablespoon dried oregano
- 1 teaspoon smoked paprika
- 1 teaspoon ground coriander
- 1 teaspoon ground cinnamon
- 1/2 teaspoon ground cloves
- Salt, to taste
- Black pepper, to taste

For the Tacos:

- 2 pounds pork shoulder, thinly sliced
- 1/2 cup white vinegar
- 1/4 cup vegetable oil
- 1/4 cup orange juice
- 1/4 cup lime juice
- 1/2 cup chopped fresh cilantro
- 1/2 cup chopped fresh pineapple
- Corn tortillas, for serving
- Diced onion, chopped cilantro, lime wedges, and salsa, for serving

Instructions:

1. In a bowl, combine the dried guajillo chilies, dried ancho chilies, pineapple juice, minced garlic, ground cumin, dried oregano, smoked paprika, ground coriander, ground cinnamon, ground cloves, salt, and black pepper. Stir well to combine.
2. Place the marinade ingredients in a blender and blend until smooth. If needed, add a little water to achieve a smooth consistency.
3. Place the thinly sliced pork shoulder in a large resealable plastic bag or shallow dish. Pour the marinade over the pork, making sure it's evenly coated. Seal the bag or cover the dish and refrigerate for at least 4 hours, or overnight for best results.
4. Preheat your grill to medium-high heat or preheat the broiler in your oven.
5. In a small bowl, whisk together the white vinegar, vegetable oil, orange juice, and lime juice to make a basting sauce.
6. Thread the marinated pork slices onto skewers or a vertical rotisserie spit. If using skewers, make sure to thread the pork slices tightly together to form a compact cylinder.
7. Grill the pork skewers or cook them under the broiler, basting occasionally with the prepared sauce, until the pork is cooked through and slightly charred on the edges, about 10-12 minutes.
8. Remove the cooked pork from the skewers and transfer it to a cutting board. Use a sharp knife to thinly slice the pork.
9. Warm the corn tortillas on the grill or in a skillet until soft and pliable.
10. To assemble the tacos, place some sliced pork onto each warm tortilla. Top with chopped fresh cilantro, chopped fresh pineapple, diced onion, and a squeeze of lime juice. Serve with your favorite salsa on the side.
11. Enjoy your homemade Tacos al Pastor, a flavorful and authentic Mexican dish that's perfect for any occasion!

Indian Vegetable Biryani

Ingredients:

For the Rice:

- 2 cups basmati rice
- 4 cups water
- Salt, to taste

For the Vegetable Mixture:

- 2 tablespoons ghee or vegetable oil
- 1 large onion, thinly sliced
- 2 cloves garlic, minced
- 1-inch piece of ginger, minced
- 2 green chilies, slit lengthwise (adjust to taste)
- 2 medium tomatoes, diced
- 2 cups mixed vegetables (such as carrots, peas, beans, cauliflower), chopped
- 1/2 cup plain yogurt
- 1 teaspoon ground turmeric
- 1 teaspoon ground cumin
- 1 teaspoon ground coriander
- 1/2 teaspoon garam masala
- Salt, to taste
- Fresh cilantro, chopped, for garnish

For Layering:

- Saffron threads (optional)
- Warm milk (optional)
- Ghee or melted butter

Instructions:

1. Rinse the basmati rice under cold water until the water runs clear. Soak the rice in water for 30 minutes, then drain.
2. In a large pot, bring 4 cups of water to a boil. Add salt to taste. Add the soaked and drained rice to the boiling water. Cook the rice until it is 70% cooked, about 6-8 minutes. Drain the rice and set it aside.
3. In a large skillet or Dutch oven, heat ghee or vegetable oil over medium heat. Add the thinly sliced onion and sauté until golden brown and caramelized, about 8-10 minutes.
4. Add minced garlic, minced ginger, and slit green chilies to the skillet. Sauté for another 2 minutes until fragrant.
5. Add diced tomatoes to the skillet and cook until they are softened, about 5 minutes.
6. Stir in the mixed vegetables and cook for 5-7 minutes until they are slightly tender.
7. Add plain yogurt, ground turmeric, ground cumin, ground coriander, garam masala, and salt to taste. Mix well to combine and cook for another 2-3 minutes.
8. Preheat your oven to 350°F (180°C).
9. In a large baking dish, layer half of the cooked rice. Spread the vegetable mixture evenly over the rice layer. Top with the remaining rice, spreading it out evenly.
10. If using saffron, soak a few saffron threads in warm milk for 10 minutes. Drizzle the saffron-infused milk over the top layer of rice. Drizzle some ghee or melted butter over the rice as well.
11. Cover the baking dish with aluminum foil and bake in the preheated oven for 20-25 minutes, or until the rice is fully cooked and fluffy.
12. Once done, remove the biryani from the oven and let it sit for 5 minutes. Garnish with fresh chopped cilantro before serving.
13. Serve the Vegetable Biryani hot with raita (yogurt sauce), pickle, or salad on the side.
14. Enjoy your homemade Indian Vegetable Biryani, a delicious and satisfying rice dish filled with aromatic flavors and colorful vegetables!

French Croque Monsieur

Ingredients:

- 8 slices of white bread (sliced about 1/2-inch thick)
- 4 tablespoons unsalted butter, softened
- 8 slices of cooked ham
- 8 slices of Gruyère cheese (or Emmental cheese)
- Dijon mustard, for spreading (optional)

For the Béchamel Sauce:

- 2 tablespoons unsalted butter
- 2 tablespoons all-purpose flour
- 1 cup whole milk
- 1/4 teaspoon salt
- 1/4 teaspoon black pepper
- Pinch of nutmeg

Instructions:

1. Preheat your oven to 400°F (200°C).
2. To make the béchamel sauce, melt 2 tablespoons of butter in a saucepan over medium heat. Add the flour and whisk constantly for about 1-2 minutes to make a roux.
3. Gradually pour in the milk, whisking constantly to prevent lumps from forming. Cook the sauce until it thickens and comes to a gentle boil, about 3-4 minutes.
4. Remove the saucepan from the heat and stir in the salt, black pepper, and a pinch of nutmeg. Set the béchamel sauce aside.
5. Spread a thin layer of Dijon mustard (if using) on 4 slices of bread. Place a slice of ham on each of the mustard-coated bread slices.
6. Top each slice of ham with a slice of Gruyère cheese.
7. Spread a generous amount of béchamel sauce over the remaining 4 slices of bread. Place the sauce-coated bread slices on top of the cheese slices to form sandwiches.
8. Spread a thin layer of softened butter on the outsides of each sandwich.

9. Heat a large skillet or griddle over medium heat. Place the sandwiches in the skillet and cook until golden brown and crispy on both sides, about 3-4 minutes per side.
10. Once the sandwiches are golden brown, transfer them to a baking sheet lined with parchment paper.
11. Spread a little more béchamel sauce on top of each sandwich and sprinkle with some additional Gruyère cheese.
12. Place the baking sheet in the preheated oven and bake for about 5-7 minutes, or until the cheese is melted and bubbly.
13. Remove the Croque Monsieur from the oven and let them cool for a few minutes before serving.
14. Serve the French Croque Monsieur sandwiches hot, with a side salad or pickles if desired.
15. Enjoy your homemade Croque Monsieur, a delicious and satisfying French sandwich perfect for lunch or a casual dinner!

Greek Moussaka

Ingredients:

For the Eggplant Layers:

- 2-3 large eggplants, sliced into 1/4-inch rounds
- Salt, for sweating the eggplant
- Olive oil, for brushing the eggplant slices
- All-purpose flour, for dusting the eggplant slices
- Ground black pepper, to taste

For the Meat Sauce:

- 1 tablespoon olive oil
- 1 onion, finely chopped
- 2 cloves garlic, minced
- 1 pound ground lamb or beef
- 1 can (14.5 ounces) diced tomatoes
- 2 tablespoons tomato paste
- 1 teaspoon dried oregano
- 1 teaspoon dried thyme
- 1/2 teaspoon ground cinnamon
- Salt and black pepper, to taste

For the Béchamel Sauce:

- 4 tablespoons unsalted butter
- 1/4 cup all-purpose flour
- 2 cups whole milk
- Pinch of nutmeg
- Salt and black pepper, to taste
- 2 large eggs
- 1/2 cup grated Parmesan cheese

Instructions:

1. Preheat your oven to 400°F (200°C).
2. Place the sliced eggplant rounds in a colander and sprinkle them with salt. Let them sit for about 30 minutes to release excess moisture. Rinse the eggplant slices under cold water and pat them dry with paper towels.
3. Arrange the eggplant slices on baking sheets. Brush both sides of the eggplant slices with olive oil and sprinkle them with black pepper. Dust the slices lightly with flour.
4. Bake the eggplant slices in the preheated oven for about 15-20 minutes, or until they are golden brown and tender. Remove them from the oven and set aside.
5. While the eggplant is baking, prepare the meat sauce. Heat olive oil in a large skillet over medium heat. Add the chopped onion and minced garlic, and cook until softened, about 5 minutes.
6. Add the ground lamb or beef to the skillet and cook until browned, breaking up any clumps with a spoon.
7. Stir in the diced tomatoes, tomato paste, dried oregano, dried thyme, ground cinnamon, salt, and black pepper. Simmer the sauce for about 10-15 minutes, or until thickened. Remove from heat and set aside.
8. To make the béchamel sauce, melt butter in a saucepan over medium heat. Add flour and whisk constantly for about 1-2 minutes to make a roux.
9. Gradually pour in the milk, whisking constantly to prevent lumps from forming. Cook the sauce until it thickens and comes to a gentle boil, about 3-4 minutes.
10. Remove the saucepan from the heat and stir in the nutmeg, salt, and black pepper. Let the sauce cool slightly.
11. In a small bowl, lightly beat the eggs. Gradually whisk the beaten eggs into the warm béchamel sauce until smooth. Stir in the grated Parmesan cheese.
12. Grease a baking dish with olive oil. Arrange half of the baked eggplant slices in an even layer on the bottom of the dish.
13. Spread the meat sauce evenly over the eggplant layer.
14. Top the meat sauce with the remaining eggplant slices.
15. Pour the béchamel sauce over the top of the eggplant layers, spreading it out evenly with a spatula.
16. Bake the moussaka in the preheated oven for about 40-45 minutes, or until the top is golden brown and bubbly.
17. Remove the moussaka from the oven and let it cool for a few minutes before slicing and serving.

18. Serve the Greek Moussaka warm, garnished with chopped fresh parsley if desired.
19. Enjoy your homemade Greek Moussaka, a hearty and comforting dish that's perfect for sharing with family and friends!

Chinese Dumplings (Potstickers)

Ingredients:

For the Dumpling Filling:

- 1/2 pound ground pork
- 1 cup finely chopped cabbage
- 2 green onions, finely chopped
- 2 cloves garlic, minced
- 1 tablespoon ginger, minced
- 1 tablespoon soy sauce
- 1 teaspoon sesame oil
- 1/2 teaspoon salt
- 1/4 teaspoon black pepper
- Optional: 1/4 cup chopped cilantro, 1/4 cup chopped shrimp

For the Dumpling Wrapper:

- Round dumpling wrappers (you can find these in the refrigerated section of most Asian grocery stores)

For Cooking:

- Vegetable oil
- Water

Instructions:

1. In a large mixing bowl, combine the ground pork, chopped cabbage, green onions, garlic, ginger, soy sauce, sesame oil, salt, and black pepper. Mix well until all the ingredients are evenly incorporated. If using, add chopped cilantro and shrimp.
2. To assemble the dumplings, place a small spoonful of the filling in the center of a dumpling wrapper. Dip your finger in water and moisten the edges of the wrapper.

Fold the wrapper in half to form a half-moon shape, then pinch the edges together to seal. You can also crimp the edges for a decorative touch.
3. Repeat the process until all the filling is used up, covering the assembled dumplings with a damp cloth or plastic wrap to prevent them from drying out.
4. To cook the dumplings, heat a tablespoon of vegetable oil in a large non-stick skillet over medium-high heat. Once the oil is hot, arrange the dumplings in the skillet in a single layer, making sure they're not touching each other.
5. Cook the dumplings for 2-3 minutes, or until the bottoms are golden brown and crispy.
6. Carefully pour enough water into the skillet to come halfway up the sides of the dumplings. Be cautious as the oil may splatter.
7. Cover the skillet with a lid and reduce the heat to medium-low. Let the dumplings steam for 6-8 minutes, or until the wrappers are translucent and the filling is cooked through.
8. Remove the lid and let any remaining water evaporate. Continue to cook the dumplings uncovered for another 1-2 minutes, or until the bottoms are crispy again.
9. Once cooked, transfer the dumplings to a serving platter.
10. Serve the Chinese dumplings hot with your favorite dipping sauce, such as soy sauce mixed with a splash of rice vinegar and a pinch of sugar, or chili oil.
11. Enjoy your homemade Chinese dumplings (potstickers), a delightful appetizer or main course bursting with flavor!

Lebanese Tabbouleh

Ingredients:

- 1/2 cup bulgur wheat
- 1 cup boiling water
- 3 cups finely chopped fresh parsley (about 2 large bunches)
- 1 cup finely chopped fresh mint leaves
- 2 medium tomatoes, diced
- 1/2 cup finely chopped red onion
- 1/4 cup extra-virgin olive oil
- 1/4 cup fresh lemon juice (about 2 lemons)
- Salt and black pepper, to taste

Instructions:

1. Place the bulgur wheat in a heatproof bowl. Pour the boiling water over the bulgur, cover, and let it sit for about 15-20 minutes, or until the bulgur is tender and has absorbed all the water. Fluff the bulgur with a fork and let it cool to room temperature.
2. In a large mixing bowl, combine the chopped parsley, chopped mint, diced tomatoes, and chopped red onion.
3. Add the cooked and cooled bulgur wheat to the bowl with the vegetables.
4. In a small bowl, whisk together the extra-virgin olive oil and fresh lemon juice to make the dressing. Season with salt and black pepper to taste.
5. Pour the dressing over the tabbouleh salad and toss well to combine, ensuring all the ingredients are evenly coated.
6. Taste the tabbouleh and adjust the seasoning if needed, adding more salt, pepper, or lemon juice to taste.
7. Cover the tabbouleh and refrigerate for at least 30 minutes to allow the flavors to meld together.
8. Before serving, give the tabbouleh a final toss and adjust the seasoning if needed.
9. Serve the Lebanese Tabbouleh as a refreshing salad or as a side dish to accompany grilled meats, fish, or falafel.
10. Enjoy your homemade Lebanese Tabbouleh, a vibrant and flavorful dish that's perfect for warm weather gatherings or as a light and healthy meal!

Brazilian Coxinha (Chicken Croquettes)

Ingredients:

For the Filling:

- 2 boneless, skinless chicken breasts
- 1 small onion, chopped
- 2 cloves garlic, minced
- 1 bay leaf
- Salt and pepper, to taste
- Water, for boiling

For the Dough:

- 2 cups chicken broth (reserved from boiling the chicken)
- 2 tablespoons unsalted butter
- 2 cups all-purpose flour
- Salt, to taste

For Breading and Frying:

- 2 large eggs, beaten
- 1 cup fine breadcrumbs
- Vegetable oil, for frying

Instructions:

1. In a large saucepan, combine the chicken breasts, chopped onion, minced garlic, bay leaf, salt, and pepper. Cover with water and bring to a boil over medium-high heat.
2. Reduce the heat to low and simmer for about 20-25 minutes, or until the chicken is cooked through and tender.

3. Remove the chicken from the broth and let it cool slightly. Shred the chicken using two forks or your fingers. Set aside.
4. In a separate saucepan, bring the chicken broth and unsalted butter to a boil over medium heat.
5. Reduce the heat to low and gradually add the flour to the saucepan, stirring constantly with a wooden spoon until a dough forms. Cook the dough for 2-3 minutes, stirring constantly, until it pulls away from the sides of the pan.
6. Remove the dough from the heat and transfer it to a lightly floured surface. Knead the dough for a few minutes until smooth and elastic. Let it cool slightly.
7. Take a small portion of the dough (about the size of a golf ball) and flatten it in your palm. Place a spoonful of the shredded chicken filling in the center of the dough.
8. Fold the dough over the filling to encase it completely, shaping it into a teardrop or drumstick shape. Seal the edges tightly to prevent the filling from leaking out.
9. Repeat the process with the remaining dough and filling.
10. Dip each coxinha into the beaten eggs, then roll it in the breadcrumbs until evenly coated.
11. Heat vegetable oil in a deep fryer or large saucepan to 350°F (180°C).
12. Carefully add the coxinhas to the hot oil in batches, making sure not to overcrowd the pan. Fry for 5-6 minutes, or until golden brown and crispy.
13. Remove the coxinhas from the oil using a slotted spoon and drain them on paper towels to remove excess oil.
14. Serve the Brazilian Coxinhas hot as a delicious appetizer or snack.
15. Enjoy your homemade Coxinhas, filled with savory shredded chicken and crispy fried dough, a popular Brazilian treat perfect for any occasion!

Moroccan Couscous

Ingredients:

- 1 1/2 cups couscous
- 1 1/2 cups chicken or vegetable broth
- 2 tablespoons olive oil
- 1 onion, finely chopped
- 2 cloves garlic, minced
- 1 teaspoon ground cumin
- 1 teaspoon ground coriander
- 1 teaspoon ground cinnamon
- 1/2 teaspoon ground turmeric
- 1/2 teaspoon paprika
- Salt and black pepper, to taste
- 1 carrot, diced
- 1 zucchini, diced
- 1 red bell pepper, diced
- 1 can (15 ounces) chickpeas, drained and rinsed
- 1/4 cup chopped fresh cilantro or parsley
- Lemon wedges, for serving

Instructions:

1. Place the couscous in a large bowl. In a separate saucepan, heat the chicken or vegetable broth until it comes to a boil. Pour the boiling broth over the couscous, cover the bowl with a lid or plastic wrap, and let it sit for about 5 minutes, or until the couscous has absorbed the liquid. Fluff the couscous with a fork to separate the grains.
2. In a large skillet or frying pan, heat the olive oil over medium heat. Add the chopped onion and cook until softened, about 3-4 minutes. Add the minced garlic, ground cumin, ground coriander, ground cinnamon, ground turmeric, paprika, salt, and black pepper. Cook for an additional 1-2 minutes, stirring constantly, until the spices are fragrant.
3. Add the diced carrot, zucchini, and red bell pepper to the skillet. Cook for 5-6 minutes, or until the vegetables are tender but still crisp.

4. Stir in the cooked couscous and drained chickpeas, mixing well to combine. Cook for another 2-3 minutes, allowing the flavors to meld together.
5. Remove the skillet from the heat and stir in the chopped fresh cilantro or parsley.
6. Serve the Moroccan couscous hot, garnished with lemon wedges for squeezing over the couscous before eating.
7. Enjoy your homemade Moroccan couscous as a flavorful and satisfying main dish or side dish!

Feel free to customize this recipe by adding other vegetables, such as diced tomatoes, chopped spinach, or sliced mushrooms, and adjust the spices according to your taste preferences. You can also add cooked chicken, lamb, or seafood for a heartier meal.

Korean Kimchi

Ingredients:

- 1 head Napa cabbage
- 1/4 cup coarse sea salt
- 4 cups water
- 1 tablespoon grated ginger
- 3 cloves garlic, minced
- 2 tablespoons fish sauce (or soy sauce for a vegetarian version)
- 1 tablespoon sugar
- 3 tablespoons Korean red pepper flakes (gochugaru) or to taste
- 4 green onions, chopped
- 1 large carrot, julienned
- Optional: daikon radish, julienned

Instructions:

1. Cut the Napa cabbage lengthwise into quarters and remove the core. Then cut the quarters crosswise into 2-inch pieces.
2. Dissolve the coarse sea salt in the water in a large bowl or container. Submerge the cabbage pieces in the salt water and let them soak for about 2 hours, flipping them occasionally to ensure even salting.
3. Rinse the salted cabbage under cold water and drain thoroughly in a colander for about 30 minutes.
4. In a separate bowl, mix together the grated ginger, minced garlic, fish sauce (or soy sauce), sugar, and Korean red pepper flakes to make the kimchi paste.
5. Once the cabbage is drained, gently squeeze out any excess water and transfer it to a large mixing bowl. Add the chopped green onions, julienned carrot, and any other optional vegetables.
6. Pour the kimchi paste over the vegetables and mix well, ensuring that all the vegetables are evenly coated with the paste.
7. Pack the kimchi tightly into clean glass jars, pressing down firmly to remove any air bubbles. Leave about an inch of space at the top of each jar.
8. Seal the jars with lids and let them sit at room temperature for 1-2 days to ferment. After that, transfer the jars to the refrigerator and let the kimchi continue

to ferment for another 5-7 days before eating. The longer it ferments, the more tangy and flavorful it will become.
9. Once the kimchi has fermented to your liking, it's ready to serve! Enjoy it as a side dish, topping for rice or noodles, or as an ingredient in various Korean dishes.
10. Store any leftover kimchi in the refrigerator, where it will continue to ferment slowly and develop more flavor over time.

Note: Traditional Korean kimchi recipes may vary depending on regional preferences and family traditions. Feel free to adjust the ingredients and seasonings to suit your taste.

Spanish Gazpacho

Ingredients:

- 6 ripe tomatoes, cored and chopped
- 1 cucumber, peeled and chopped
- 1 red bell pepper, seeded and chopped
- 1 green bell pepper, seeded and chopped
- 1 small red onion, chopped
- 2 cloves garlic, minced
- 2 slices day-old bread, crusts removed
- 1/4 cup extra virgin olive oil
- 2 tablespoons red wine vinegar
- 1 teaspoon salt, or to taste
- 1/4 teaspoon black pepper, or to taste
- 1 cup cold water, or more as needed
- Optional garnishes: chopped cucumber, bell pepper, red onion, croutons, fresh herbs (such as parsley or basil), and a drizzle of olive oil

Instructions:

1. In a large bowl, combine the chopped tomatoes, cucumber, red bell pepper, green bell pepper, red onion, and minced garlic.
2. Tear the day-old bread into small pieces and add them to the bowl with the vegetables.
3. Drizzle the extra virgin olive oil and red wine vinegar over the vegetables and bread. Sprinkle with salt and black pepper.
4. Using an immersion blender or regular blender, blend the mixture until smooth and creamy. If the gazpacho is too thick, add cold water, a little at a time, until you reach your desired consistency.
5. Taste the gazpacho and adjust the seasoning, adding more salt, pepper, or vinegar if needed.
6. Cover the bowl with plastic wrap and refrigerate the gazpacho for at least 2 hours, or until well chilled.
7. Before serving, give the gazpacho a good stir. If it has thickened too much, you can thin it out with a little more cold water.
8. Ladle the chilled gazpacho into bowls and garnish with chopped cucumber, bell pepper, red onion, croutons, fresh herbs, and a drizzle of olive oil, if desired.

9. Serve the Spanish gazpacho cold as a refreshing appetizer or light meal, especially on hot summer days.
10. Enjoy your homemade Spanish gazpacho, a delicious and healthy dish bursting with the flavors of ripe vegetables and aromatic olive oil!

Vietnamese Banh Mi

Ingredients:

For the Baguette:

- 4 small Vietnamese baguettes or French baguettes, split lengthwise
- Butter or mayonnaise, for spreading

For the Filling:

- 1 pound cooked protein (such as grilled pork, shredded chicken, tofu, or beef)
- 1/2 cup pickled vegetables (carrots, daikon radish, cucumber, or other crunchy veggies)
- Fresh cilantro sprigs
- Thinly sliced jalapeños or other chili peppers (optional)
- Sliced cucumbers (optional)

For the Pickled Vegetables:

- 1 cup julienned carrots
- 1 cup julienned daikon radish
- 1/2 cup rice vinegar
- 1/4 cup water
- 2 tablespoons sugar
- 1 teaspoon salt

For the Sauce:

- 1/4 cup mayonnaise
- 2 tablespoons Sriracha sauce or to taste
- 1 tablespoon soy sauce
- 1 tablespoon honey or sugar

Instructions:

1. Prepare the pickled vegetables: In a small saucepan, combine the rice vinegar, water, sugar, and salt. Heat over medium heat until the sugar and salt are dissolved. Remove from heat and let the brine cool slightly.
2. Place the julienned carrots and daikon radish in a clean jar or bowl. Pour the warm brine over the vegetables, making sure they are completely submerged. Let the pickled vegetables sit at room temperature for at least 30 minutes, or refrigerate for longer storage.
3. Prepare the sauce: In a small bowl, whisk together the mayonnaise, Sriracha sauce, soy sauce, and honey (or sugar) until smooth. Adjust the Sriracha sauce to taste for desired spiciness.
4. Assemble the Banh Mi sandwiches: Spread butter or mayonnaise on the inside of each baguette half. Layer the cooked protein, pickled vegetables, fresh cilantro, sliced jalapeños (if using), and sliced cucumbers (if using) inside the baguette.
5. Drizzle the prepared sauce over the filling ingredients.
6. Close the baguette halves to form sandwiches.
7. Serve the Banh Mi sandwiches immediately, or wrap them tightly in parchment paper or foil for later enjoyment.
8. Enjoy your homemade Vietnamese Banh Mi sandwiches, filled with a delicious combination of flavors and textures!

Feel free to customize your Banh Mi sandwiches with additional ingredients such as sliced avocado, pâté, fried eggs, or different types of protein to suit your taste preferences.

Turkish Kofta Kebabs

Ingredients:

For the kofta:

- 1 pound ground lamb or beef (or a mixture of both)
- 1 small onion, grated
- 2 cloves garlic, minced
- 1/4 cup fresh parsley, finely chopped
- 1 teaspoon ground cumin
- 1 teaspoon paprika
- 1/2 teaspoon ground coriander
- 1/2 teaspoon ground cinnamon
- 1/4 teaspoon cayenne pepper (optional)
- Salt and black pepper, to taste
- Olive oil, for brushing

For serving:

- Flatbread or pita bread
- Sliced tomatoes
- Sliced cucumbers
- Finely chopped onions
- Fresh parsley or mint leaves
- Yogurt sauce or tzatziki

Instructions:

1. In a large mixing bowl, combine the ground meat, grated onion, minced garlic, chopped parsley, ground cumin, paprika, ground coriander, ground cinnamon, cayenne pepper (if using), salt, and black pepper. Mix well to combine all the ingredients evenly.

2. Divide the meat mixture into equal portions and shape each portion into a cylindrical sausage shape around metal skewers or bamboo skewers that have been soaked in water for at least 30 minutes.
3. Preheat a grill or grill pan over medium-high heat. Brush the kofta kebabs with olive oil on all sides.
4. Place the kofta kebabs on the grill and cook for 4-5 minutes on each side, or until they are browned and cooked through. Make sure to rotate them occasionally for even cooking.
5. While the kofta kebabs are cooking, you can prepare the serving ingredients. Warm the flatbread or pita bread on the grill for a minute or so on each side.
6. Once the kofta kebabs are cooked, remove them from the grill and let them rest for a few minutes.
7. To serve, place a piece of flatbread or pita bread on a plate. Slide the kofta kebabs off the skewers and onto the bread. Top with sliced tomatoes, cucumbers, chopped onions, and fresh parsley or mint leaves.
8. Drizzle yogurt sauce or tzatziki over the kofta kebabs.
9. Serve the Turkish kofta kebabs immediately while they are still warm.
10. Enjoy your homemade Turkish kofta kebabs, a delicious and flavorful dish perfect for a barbecue or any occasion!

Jamaican Ackee and Saltfish

Ingredients:

- 1 pound salted codfish (boneless and skinless)
- 2 cans (20 ounces) canned ackee fruit, drained and rinsed
- 2 tablespoons vegetable oil or butter
- 1 large onion, chopped
- 2 cloves garlic, minced
- 1 bell pepper (any color), chopped
- 2 tomatoes, chopped
- 2-3 Scotch bonnet peppers or habanero peppers, seeded and minced (adjust to taste)
- 1 teaspoon fresh thyme leaves
- 1/2 teaspoon ground black pepper
- 1/4 teaspoon ground allspice
- 1/4 teaspoon paprika
- Salt, to taste
- Fresh parsley or cilantro, chopped (for garnish)
- Serve with boiled green bananas, yams, dumplings, or rice (optional)

Instructions:

1. Start by soaking the salted codfish in cold water overnight or for at least 8 hours, changing the water several times to remove excess salt. Once soaked, drain the codfish and rinse it under cold water.
2. In a large pot, cover the codfish with fresh water and bring it to a boil. Reduce the heat and simmer for about 15-20 minutes, or until the codfish is tender and can be easily flaked with a fork. Drain the codfish and let it cool slightly. Flake the codfish into bite-sized pieces, removing any bones if necessary.
3. In a large skillet or frying pan, heat the vegetable oil or butter over medium heat. Add the chopped onion and cook until softened, about 3-4 minutes.
4. Add the minced garlic and cook for another minute until fragrant.
5. Stir in the chopped bell pepper, tomatoes, and minced Scotch bonnet peppers. Cook for 2-3 minutes, or until the vegetables are softened.
6. Add the flaked codfish to the skillet along with the fresh thyme leaves, ground black pepper, ground allspice, and paprika. Stir well to combine.

7. Gently fold in the drained and rinsed ackee fruit, being careful not to break up the ackee too much. Cook for an additional 3-4 minutes, or until the ackee is heated through.
8. Taste the ackee and saltfish mixture and adjust the seasoning with salt if necessary.
9. Remove the skillet from the heat and transfer the Jamaican Ackee and Saltfish to a serving dish.
10. Garnish with chopped fresh parsley or cilantro.
11. Serve the Jamaican Ackee and Saltfish hot with boiled green bananas, yams, dumplings, or rice, if desired.
12. Enjoy your homemade Jamaican Ackee and Saltfish, a delicious and flavorful dish that's perfect for breakfast, brunch, or any meal of the day!

Russian Pelmeni (Meat Dumplings)

Ingredients:

For the dough:

- 2 cups all-purpose flour, plus extra for dusting
- 2/3 cup water
- 1 egg
- 1/2 teaspoon salt

For the filling:

- 1/2 pound ground beef
- 1/2 pound ground pork
- 1 small onion, finely chopped
- 2 cloves garlic, minced
- 1 teaspoon salt
- 1/2 teaspoon black pepper
- 1/2 teaspoon ground coriander
- 1/2 teaspoon ground cumin
- 1/4 teaspoon ground nutmeg
- 1/4 teaspoon paprika
- Optional: chopped fresh parsley or dill for garnish

For serving:

- Sour cream
- Vinegar
- Soy sauce
- Mustard
- Hot sauce

Instructions:

1. In a large mixing bowl, combine the flour and salt. Make a well in the center and add the water and egg. Use a fork to gradually incorporate the flour into the wet ingredients until a dough forms.
2. Transfer the dough to a lightly floured surface and knead for about 5-7 minutes, or until smooth and elastic. Wrap the dough in plastic wrap and let it rest at room temperature for 30 minutes.
3. While the dough is resting, prepare the filling. In a separate mixing bowl, combine the ground beef, ground pork, chopped onion, minced garlic, salt, black pepper, ground coriander, ground cumin, ground nutmeg, and paprika. Mix well until all the ingredients are evenly incorporated.
4. After the dough has rested, divide it into four equal portions. Roll out one portion of dough on a lightly floured surface until it is about 1/16 inch thick. Use a round cookie cutter or the rim of a glass to cut out circles of dough, each about 2 inches in diameter.
5. Place a small amount of filling (about 1 teaspoon) in the center of each dough circle. Fold the dough over the filling to create a half-moon shape, then pinch the edges together firmly to seal.
6. Repeat the process with the remaining dough and filling, re-rolling any scraps of dough as needed.
7. Bring a large pot of salted water to a boil. Carefully drop the pelmeni into the boiling water, working in batches to avoid overcrowding the pot. Cook for about 5-7 minutes, or until the pelmeni float to the surface and are cooked through.
8. Use a slotted spoon to transfer the cooked pelmeni to a serving dish. Repeat with the remaining pelmeni.
9. Serve the pelmeni hot, garnished with chopped fresh parsley or dill if desired. Offer sour cream, vinegar, soy sauce, mustard, and hot sauce on the side for dipping or drizzling.
10. Enjoy your homemade Russian pelmeni, a delicious and comforting dish that's perfect for sharing with family and friends!

Ethiopian Injera (Sourdough Flatbread)

Ingredients:

- 2 cups teff flour (white or brown)
- 3 cups water
- 1/4 teaspoon active dry yeast (optional, for faster fermentation)
- 1/2 teaspoon salt

Instructions:

1. In a large mixing bowl, combine the teff flour and water. Stir well to form a smooth batter. If using, sprinkle the active dry yeast over the batter and mix it in thoroughly. Cover the bowl with a clean cloth and let it ferment at room temperature for 24 to 48 hours. During fermentation, the batter will develop bubbles and become slightly sour.
2. After fermentation, stir the batter and add salt. Adjust the consistency of the batter by adding more water if it is too thick. The batter should have a pourable consistency, similar to pancake batter.
3. Preheat a non-stick skillet or injera pan over medium-low heat. Lightly grease the skillet with oil or cooking spray.
4. Pour a ladleful of the batter onto the skillet, starting from the center and working your way outwards in a circular motion to form a large, thin pancake. The injera should be about 1/4 inch thick.
5. Cover the skillet with a lid and cook the injera for 2 to 3 minutes, or until bubbles form on the surface and the edges begin to lift slightly.
6. Remove the lid and cook the injera for an additional 1 to 2 minutes, or until the bottom is lightly browned and the injera is cooked through.
7. Carefully transfer the cooked injera to a plate and cover it with a clean cloth to keep it warm while you cook the remaining batter. Repeat the process with the remaining batter, greasing the skillet between each batch.
8. Serve the injera warm with your favorite Ethiopian dishes, such as doro wat (chicken stew), misir wat (spicy lentil stew), or gomen (spiced collard greens). To eat, tear off pieces of injera and use them to scoop up the accompanying dishes.
9. Enjoy your homemade Ethiopian injera, a delicious and nutritious flatbread that's perfect for sharing with family and friends!

Australian Meat Pie

Ingredients:

For the pastry:

- 2 1/2 cups all-purpose flour
- 1 teaspoon salt
- 1 cup unsalted butter, cold and cubed
- 6-8 tablespoons ice water

For the filling:

- 1 tablespoon olive oil
- 1 onion, finely chopped
- 2 cloves garlic, minced
- 1 pound ground beef or lamb
- 2 tablespoons all-purpose flour
- 1 cup beef or vegetable broth
- 1 tablespoon Worcestershire sauce
- 1 teaspoon tomato paste
- Salt and pepper, to taste
- Optional: chopped fresh herbs (such as thyme or rosemary)

Instructions:

1. Start by making the pastry. In a large mixing bowl, combine the flour and salt. Add the cold cubed butter and use a pastry cutter or your fingers to rub the butter into the flour until the mixture resembles coarse crumbs.
2. Gradually add the ice water, one tablespoon at a time, and mix until the dough comes together. Be careful not to overwork the dough. Shape the dough into a ball, wrap it in plastic wrap, and refrigerate for at least 30 minutes.
3. While the pastry chills, prepare the filling. Heat the olive oil in a large skillet over medium heat. Add the chopped onion and garlic, and cook until softened, about 3-4 minutes.

4. Add the ground beef or lamb to the skillet and cook until browned, breaking up any clumps with a spoon.
5. Sprinkle the flour over the meat mixture and stir to combine. Cook for 1-2 minutes to cook off the raw flour taste.
6. Slowly pour in the beef or vegetable broth, stirring constantly to prevent lumps from forming. Add the Worcestershire sauce, tomato paste, salt, pepper, and chopped fresh herbs (if using). Bring the mixture to a simmer and cook for 5-7 minutes, or until thickened. Remove from heat and let cool slightly.
7. Preheat your oven to 400°F (200°C). Lightly grease a 12-cup muffin tin.
8. On a lightly floured surface, roll out the chilled pastry dough to about 1/8 inch thickness. Use a round cutter or a drinking glass to cut out circles slightly larger than the size of your muffin tin cups.
9. Line each muffin tin cup with a circle of pastry dough, gently pressing it into the bottom and sides.
10. Spoon the cooled meat filling into each pastry-lined cup, filling them almost to the top.
11. Roll out the remaining pastry dough and cut out slightly smaller circles to use as tops for the pies. Place a pastry circle over each filled cup and press the edges to seal.
12. Use a sharp knife to cut a small slit in the center of each pie to allow steam to escape.
13. Bake the pies in the preheated oven for 20-25 minutes, or until the pastry is golden brown and crisp.
14. Remove the pies from the oven and let them cool in the muffin tin for a few minutes before transferring them to a wire rack to cool completely.
15. Serve the Australian meat pies warm, optionally with tomato sauce (ketchup) on the side.
16. Enjoy your homemade Australian meat pies, a delicious and comforting savory treat!

Peruvian Lomo Saltado

Ingredients:

For the marinade:

- 1 pound beef sirloin, thinly sliced
- 2 cloves garlic, minced
- 2 tablespoons soy sauce
- 1 tablespoon red wine vinegar
- 1 teaspoon ground cumin
- 1 teaspoon paprika
- Salt and pepper, to taste

For the stir-fry:

- 2 tablespoons vegetable oil
- 1 onion, thinly sliced
- 1 red bell pepper, thinly sliced
- 1 yellow bell pepper, thinly sliced
- 2 tomatoes, cut into wedges
- 1 jalapeño pepper, thinly sliced (optional, for extra heat)
- 3 tablespoons soy sauce
- 2 tablespoons red wine vinegar
- 1 tablespoon aji amarillo paste (Peruvian yellow chili paste) or substitute with hot sauce or chili paste
- 1/4 cup chopped fresh cilantro
- Cooked white rice, for serving
- French fries, for serving (optional)

Instructions:

1. In a bowl, combine the thinly sliced beef with minced garlic, soy sauce, red wine vinegar, ground cumin, paprika, salt, and pepper. Mix well to ensure the beef is

evenly coated with the marinade. Let it marinate for at least 30 minutes, or up to overnight in the refrigerator.
2. Heat one tablespoon of vegetable oil in a large skillet or wok over high heat. Once hot, add the marinated beef in batches and stir-fry for 2-3 minutes, or until browned and cooked through. Transfer the cooked beef to a plate and set aside.
3. In the same skillet or wok, add another tablespoon of vegetable oil. Add the thinly sliced onion and bell peppers, and stir-fry for 2-3 minutes, or until the vegetables are slightly softened.
4. Add the tomato wedges and sliced jalapeño pepper (if using) to the skillet, and continue to stir-fry for another 1-2 minutes.
5. Return the cooked beef to the skillet, and add soy sauce, red wine vinegar, and aji amarillo paste (or hot sauce/chili paste). Stir well to combine all the ingredients.
6. Cook for an additional 1-2 minutes, or until everything is heated through and well combined.
7. Remove the skillet from heat and stir in the chopped fresh cilantro.
8. Serve the Peruvian Lomo Saltado hot over a bed of cooked white rice, and optionally with French fries on the side.
9. Enjoy your homemade Peruvian Lomo Saltado, a delicious and flavorful dish that combines the best of Peruvian and Chinese cuisine!

Nigerian Pounded Yam and Egusi Soup

Ingredients:

For the Pounded Yam:

- 1 pound yam (you can use yams specifically labeled as "pounded yam" if available)
- Water, for boiling

For the Egusi Soup:

- 1 cup egusi (ground melon seeds)
- 1/2 cup palm oil or vegetable oil
- 1 onion, finely chopped
- 2-3 garlic cloves, minced
- 2-3 cups chopped vegetables (such as spinach, kale, or bitterleaf)
- 1/2 cup ground crayfish
- 2 cups meat or fish stock
- 1 pound meat or fish (such as beef, chicken, goat meat, or fish fillets)
- Salt and pepper, to taste
- 1-2 scotch bonnet peppers or habanero peppers, chopped (optional, for heat)
- 1 tablespoon ground crayfish
- 1 teaspoon ground cayenne pepper (optional, for extra heat)
- 1 teaspoon dried ground bitterleaf (optional, for traditional flavor)
- 1 tablespoon dried or ground uziza leaves (optional, for extra flavor)

Instructions:

For the Pounded Yam:

1. Peel the yam and cut it into chunks. Rinse the yam chunks under cold water to remove any dirt or debris.

2. Place the yam chunks in a large pot and cover them with water. Bring the water to a boil over medium-high heat and cook the yam until tender, about 15-20 minutes.
3. Drain the cooked yam and transfer it to a mortar and pestle or a stand mixer fitted with a paddle attachment. Pound or mix the yam until it becomes smooth and stretchy, adding a little water as needed to achieve the desired consistency.
4. Once the yam is pounded, shape it into smooth balls or loaves and set aside.

For the Egusi Soup:

1. In a dry skillet, toast the egusi (ground melon seeds) over medium heat for 5-7 minutes, stirring frequently, until fragrant and slightly browned. Remove from heat and set aside.
2. In a large pot, heat the palm oil or vegetable oil over medium heat. Add the chopped onion and minced garlic, and sauté until softened and fragrant, about 2-3 minutes.
3. Add the toasted egusi to the pot and stir well to combine with the onions and garlic.
4. Gradually add the meat or fish stock to the pot, stirring continuously to prevent lumps from forming.
5. Add the chopped vegetables, ground crayfish, meat or fish (pre-cooked if using), salt, pepper, chopped scotch bonnet peppers (if using), ground cayenne pepper (if using), dried ground bitterleaf (if using), and dried or ground uziza leaves (if using). Stir well to combine.
6. Bring the soup to a simmer and cook for 20-30 minutes, stirring occasionally, until the vegetables are tender and the soup has thickened to your desired consistency.
7. Taste the soup and adjust the seasoning with more salt and pepper if needed.
8. Serve the Egusi Soup hot, accompanied by the pounded yam balls or loaves.
9. Enjoy your homemade Nigerian Pounded Yam and Egusi Soup, a delicious and comforting dish that's perfect for sharing with family and friends!

Cuban Cubano Sandwich

Ingredients:

- Cuban bread or French bread, cut into sandwich-sized pieces
- Roast pork (pernil), thinly sliced
- Ham, thinly sliced
- Swiss cheese, sliced
- Dill pickles, sliced lengthwise
- Yellow mustard
- Butter or margarine, softened

Instructions:

1. Preheat a panini press, sandwich press, or a large skillet over medium heat.
2. Slice the Cuban bread or French bread horizontally to open it up for sandwich assembly.
3. Spread mustard on the inside of both halves of the bread.
4. Layer the roast pork, ham, Swiss cheese, and pickles on one half of the bread, then close the sandwich with the other half.
5. Spread butter or margarine on the outside of the sandwich.
6. Place the sandwich on the preheated panini press, sandwich press, or skillet. If using a skillet, place another heavy skillet or a pan on top of the sandwich to press it down.
7. Cook the sandwich for 3-4 minutes on each side, or until the bread is golden brown and the cheese is melted.
8. Once cooked, remove the sandwich from the panini press, sandwich press, or skillet, and let it cool for a minute or two before slicing it diagonally.
9. Serve the Cubano sandwich hot, and enjoy the delicious combination of flavors and textures!
10. Optional: Serve with additional pickles, mustard, or a side of plantain chips for a traditional Cuban meal.
11. Enjoy your homemade Cubano sandwich, a classic and satisfying dish that's perfect for lunch or dinner!

Thai Pad Thai

Ingredients:

- 8 oz (about 225g) dried rice noodles (preferably wide or medium width)
- 2 tablespoons tamarind paste
- 2 tablespoons fish sauce
- 2 tablespoons soy sauce
- 1 tablespoon brown sugar (or palm sugar)
- 1 tablespoon vegetable oil
- 2 cloves garlic, minced
- 1 small shallot, thinly sliced
- 2 large eggs, lightly beaten
- 8 oz (about 225g) protein of choice (chicken, shrimp, tofu, or a combination)
- 1 cup bean sprouts
- 2 green onions, sliced
- 1/4 cup chopped roasted peanuts
- Lime wedges, for serving
- Cilantro leaves, for garnish
- Red chili flakes, for garnish (optional)

Instructions:

1. Cook the rice noodles according to package instructions until they are tender but still slightly firm. Drain and set aside.
2. In a small bowl, mix together the tamarind paste, fish sauce, soy sauce, and brown sugar. Set aside.
3. Heat the vegetable oil in a large skillet or wok over medium-high heat. Add the minced garlic and sliced shallots, and cook until fragrant, about 1 minute.
4. Push the garlic and shallots to one side of the skillet, and pour the beaten eggs into the empty side. Scramble the eggs until they are cooked through, then mix them with the garlic and shallots.
5. Add the protein of your choice (chicken, shrimp, tofu, or a combination) to the skillet, and cook until it is fully cooked and browned, about 2-3 minutes.
6. Add the cooked rice noodles to the skillet, along with the tamarind sauce mixture. Toss everything together until the noodles are well coated in the sauce and heated through.

7. Add the bean sprouts and sliced green onions to the skillet, and toss everything together for another 1-2 minutes, until the bean sprouts are slightly softened.
8. Remove the skillet from the heat, and sprinkle the chopped roasted peanuts over the top of the Pad Thai.
9. Serve the Pad Thai hot, garnished with lime wedges, cilantro leaves, and red chili flakes (if using).
10. Enjoy your homemade Pad Thai, a delicious and satisfying Thai noodle dish that's perfect for lunch or dinner!

Italian Risotto

Ingredients:

- 1 1/2 cups Arborio rice
- 4 cups chicken or vegetable broth
- 1/2 cup dry white wine (optional)
- 2 tablespoons unsalted butter
- 2 tablespoons olive oil
- 1 small onion, finely chopped
- 2 cloves garlic, minced
- 1/2 cup grated Parmesan cheese
- Salt and pepper, to taste
- Chopped fresh herbs (such as parsley, thyme, or basil), for garnish (optional)

Instructions:

1. In a saucepan, heat the chicken or vegetable broth over medium heat. Once heated, reduce the heat to low to keep the broth warm while you prepare the risotto.
2. In a large skillet or saucepan, heat the olive oil and butter over medium heat. Add the chopped onion and garlic, and cook until softened and translucent, about 3-4 minutes.
3. Add the Arborio rice to the skillet, and stir to coat the rice with the oil and butter. Cook for 1-2 minutes, stirring constantly, until the rice becomes slightly translucent around the edges.
4. If using, pour in the white wine and cook, stirring constantly, until the wine is absorbed by the rice.
5. Begin adding the warm broth to the skillet, one ladleful at a time, stirring constantly and allowing each addition of broth to be absorbed by the rice before adding more. Continue this process until the rice is cooked through and creamy, but still slightly firm to the bite (al dente). This should take about 18-20 minutes.
6. Once the rice is cooked to your desired consistency, stir in the grated Parmesan cheese until melted and well incorporated. Season with salt and pepper to taste.
7. Remove the risotto from the heat and let it rest for a minute or two before serving.
8. Serve the risotto hot, garnished with chopped fresh herbs if desired.

9. Enjoy your homemade Italian risotto as a delicious and comforting meal! You can also customize your risotto by adding ingredients such as mushrooms, peas, asparagus, shrimp, or pancetta for additional flavor and texture.

Japanese Tempura

Ingredients:

For the tempura batter:

- 1 cup all-purpose flour
- 1 egg, beaten
- 1 cup ice-cold water
- Pinch of salt
- Ice cubes

For the tempura:

- Assorted vegetables (such as bell peppers, sweet potatoes, onions, mushrooms, zucchini, and eggplant), cut into bite-sized pieces
- Seafood (such as shrimp, squid, or fish fillets), cleaned and deveined if necessary
- Vegetable oil, for deep-frying

For serving:

- Tempura dipping sauce (Tentsuyu), or soy sauce mixed with grated daikon radish and ginger

Instructions:

1. Prepare the tempura batter by combining the all-purpose flour, beaten egg, ice-cold water, and a pinch of salt in a mixing bowl. Mix gently until just combined. Do not overmix; it's okay if there are lumps in the batter. The key to light and crispy tempura is to keep the batter cold, so it's important to use ice-cold water and keep the batter bowl on top of ice cubes.
2. Heat the vegetable oil in a deep fryer or large pot to 350-375°F (180-190°C).
3. While the oil is heating, prepare the vegetables and seafood for frying. Pat them dry with paper towels to remove excess moisture, which helps the batter adhere better.
4. Dip the vegetables and seafood pieces into the tempura batter, coating them evenly. Allow any excess batter to drip off before adding them to the hot oil.

5. Carefully place the battered vegetables and seafood into the hot oil, making sure not to overcrowd the pot. Fry in batches if necessary to maintain the oil temperature and ensure even cooking.
6. Fry the tempura until golden brown and crispy, about 2-3 minutes for vegetables and 3-4 minutes for seafood. Use a slotted spoon or tongs to remove the tempura from the oil and transfer them to a wire rack or paper towel-lined plate to drain excess oil.
7. Serve the tempura hot, accompanied by tempura dipping sauce (Tentsuyu) or a mixture of soy sauce, grated daikon radish, and ginger for dipping.
8. Enjoy your homemade Japanese tempura as a delicious appetizer or main dish! Tempura is best served immediately after frying to maintain its crispiness.

Mexican Chiles Rellenos

Ingredients:

- 4 large poblano peppers
- 1 cup shredded cheese (such as Oaxaca cheese, Monterey Jack, or mozzarella)
- 1/2 cup all-purpose flour
- 4 large eggs, separated
- Vegetable oil, for frying
- Salt, to taste
- Optional toppings: salsa roja, salsa verde, crema, chopped cilantro, diced onions

Instructions:

1. Preheat the broiler in your oven. Place the poblano peppers on a baking sheet and broil them for 5-7 minutes, turning occasionally, until the skins are blistered and charred on all sides. Transfer the roasted peppers to a bowl and cover them with a clean kitchen towel. Let them steam for about 10 minutes to loosen the skins.
2. Once the peppers have steamed, carefully peel off the charred skins. Make a lengthwise slit down one side of each pepper and remove the seeds and membranes, taking care to keep the peppers intact.
3. Stuff each pepper with shredded cheese, then gently press the edges of the peppers together to enclose the cheese.
4. In a shallow dish, beat the egg whites until stiff peaks form. In another shallow dish, lightly beat the egg yolks.
5. Heat vegetable oil in a large skillet over medium heat.
6. Dredge each stuffed pepper in flour, shaking off any excess. Then dip each pepper into the beaten egg yolks, coating them evenly.
7. Gently fold the beaten egg whites into the remaining egg yolks to create a light and fluffy batter.
8. Carefully place the battered peppers into the hot oil and fry them until golden brown on all sides, about 3-4 minutes per side.
9. Once the peppers are cooked through and crispy, transfer them to a paper towel-lined plate to drain excess oil. Sprinkle with salt while still hot.
10. Serve the Chiles Rellenos hot, topped with your favorite salsa (salsa roja or salsa verde), crema, chopped cilantro, and diced onions.

11. Enjoy your homemade Mexican Chiles Rellenos as a delicious and satisfying meal!

Indian Palak Paneer

Ingredients:

- 2 bunches of fresh spinach (about 500g), washed and chopped
- 200g paneer, cut into cubes
- 2 tablespoons ghee or vegetable oil
- 1 onion, finely chopped
- 2 tomatoes, finely chopped
- 3 cloves garlic, minced
- 1-inch piece of ginger, grated
- 1 green chili, finely chopped (optional, adjust to taste)
- 1 teaspoon cumin seeds
- 1 teaspoon ground coriander
- 1/2 teaspoon ground turmeric
- 1/2 teaspoon garam masala
- 1/2 teaspoon ground cumin
- Salt, to taste
- 1/4 cup heavy cream or yogurt (optional)
- Fresh cilantro leaves, for garnish

Instructions:

1. Blanch the spinach: Bring a large pot of water to a boil. Add the chopped spinach and blanch for 2-3 minutes, until wilted. Drain the spinach and immediately transfer it to a bowl of ice water to stop the cooking process. Drain again and set aside.
2. Heat 1 tablespoon of ghee or vegetable oil in a large skillet or pan over medium heat. Add the paneer cubes and fry them until golden brown on all sides. Remove the paneer from the pan and set aside.
3. In the same skillet, add the remaining tablespoon of ghee or oil. Add the cumin seeds and sauté until they start to sizzle.
4. Add the chopped onion and cook until it becomes soft and translucent, about 5 minutes.
5. Add the minced garlic, grated ginger, and chopped green chili (if using). Cook for another 2 minutes, until fragrant.

6. Add the chopped tomatoes to the skillet and cook until they break down and become soft, about 5-7 minutes.
7. Add the ground coriander, ground turmeric, ground cumin, and salt to the skillet. Stir well to combine and cook for another 2-3 minutes.
8. Add the blanched spinach to the skillet and stir to combine with the tomato mixture. Cook for 5-7 minutes, allowing the flavors to meld together.
9. Transfer the spinach mixture to a blender or food processor and blend until smooth. You may need to do this in batches, depending on the size of your blender.
10. Return the blended spinach mixture to the skillet and bring it to a simmer. Add the fried paneer cubes and garam masala to the skillet. Stir well to combine and cook for another 5 minutes.
11. If using, stir in the heavy cream or yogurt to add richness to the dish. Cook for an additional 2-3 minutes, then remove the skillet from the heat.
12. Garnish the Palak Paneer with fresh cilantro leaves before serving.
13. Serve the Palak Paneer hot with naan, roti, or rice.

Enjoy your homemade Palak Paneer, a delicious and nutritious Indian dish!

French Crème Brûlée

Ingredients:

- 2 cups heavy cream
- 1/2 cup granulated sugar
- 5 large egg yolks
- 1 teaspoon vanilla extract
- Additional granulated sugar for caramelizing

Instructions:

1. Preheat your oven to 300°F (150°C). Place six ramekins in a baking dish and set aside.
2. In a saucepan, heat the heavy cream over medium heat until it just begins to simmer. Remove from heat and set aside.
3. In a mixing bowl, whisk together the granulated sugar and egg yolks until pale and creamy.
4. Gradually pour the warm cream into the egg yolk mixture, whisking constantly to prevent the eggs from scrambling.
5. Stir in the vanilla extract.
6. Strain the custard mixture through a fine-mesh sieve to remove any lumps.
7. Divide the custard mixture evenly among the ramekins.
8. Carefully pour hot water into the baking dish until it reaches about halfway up the sides of the ramekins, creating a water bath for even cooking.
9. Bake the crème brûlées in the preheated oven for 35-40 minutes, or until the custard is set around the edges but still slightly jiggly in the center.
10. Remove the ramekins from the water bath and let them cool to room temperature. Then cover and refrigerate for at least 2 hours, or until thoroughly chilled.
11. Just before serving, sprinkle a thin, even layer of granulated sugar over the top of each custard.
12. Use a kitchen torch to carefully caramelize the sugar until it forms a golden-brown crust. Alternatively, you can place the ramekins under the broiler for 1-2 minutes, watching closely to prevent burning.
13. Allow the caramelized sugar to harden for a few minutes before serving.

14. Serve the French Crème Brûlée immediately and enjoy the creamy custard with its signature crunchy caramelized topping!

Enjoy your homemade French Crème Brûlée as a decadent and elegant dessert!

www.ingramcontent.com/pod-product-compliance
Lightning Source LLC
LaVergne TN
LVHW061942070526
838199LV00060B/3924